Liz

Thank you for
all your support
and encouragement ♡

Rebecca
Mike

TESTIMONIALS

Written by two leaders in the field, this insightful and highly practical playbook is a "must read" for professionals looking to go plural and live a life of purposeful flourishing.

—Louise Chester, *Managing Director Potential Project UK and Founder at Mindfulness at Work Ltd*

This book is perfectly timed to provide practical guidance to individuals who are looking for the next chapter in their careers and want to build on their wealth of experience to create a plural career. The book is underpinned by research and the chapters are concise and with short exercises that take the reader from thinking to doing elegantly.

—Dr Shaheena Janjuha-Jivraj, *FRSA Associate Professor, HEC Paris Business School in Qatar*

As someone who has a special interest in transitions, I found this book a brilliant and practical guide to helping people navigate their next professional chapters. It's well-structured and easy to read, and I particularly liked the case studies that showed the different ways in which people are creating their encore careers and the reflective exercises which was like having a personal coach in the room.

—Lesley Salem, *Founder, Over The Bloody Moon*

This book is a portal for professionals exploring life options. Packed with practical ideas, positive insights, and inspiring case studies. Highly recommended for the fabulously 50+.

—Helene Martin Gee, *Founder, Savvitas*

As someone in the "middle of life," this book provides a much-needed nudge to stop and think. To organize our existence with an eye to the future we want to build for ourselves—instead of allowing ourselves to get lost in the whirl of our current working world.

—Beth Knight, *Community Investment Leader, Amazon Fellow, Institute of Sustainability Leadership, University of Cambridge*

This incredibly engaging book highlights the challenges that Gen-X and Boomers particularly face today as they transition into mid- and later-life. Critically, it flags the questions that we need to start asking ourselves as the world is changing—including our world of work and how we work. This book takes you on a practical journey of choice. Having known the authors for several years, they have sound knowledge and a very pragmatic approach. I believe this is a must read, no matter where you are in your career for practical insights and guidance.

—Dr Donna Johnston, *Head of Learning & Talent, Quorn Foods*

I must admit that I have so far not spent much time thinking about "encore"....I now realise that I probably should! Being prepared appears to be half the challenge. The examples and case studies discussed by the authors provide brilliant context, while the prompts for reflection and exercises offer focus and the opportunity for meticulous planning. I cannot wait to put this into practice when the time comes!

—Margot von Aesch, *Head of Sustainable Investment Management at Schroders*

A great practical read, which provides fascinating insights and advice on how to approach your professional transition from organisational life into a fulfilling encore.

—Chip Conley, *Founder, Modern Elder Academy and New York Times bestselling author*

I found the book to be a practical and easily accessible summary of the options available to those approaching their "encore career" years. Being slightly younger than the target age group—although not for long!—I wasn't sure how relevant their ideas and insights would be, but in reality, the case studies and practical tips were incredibly helpful in planning a course of action which starts now, not in 10 years' time.

—Eve Read, *Acting Director of Customer Engagement, Nest*

With practical, actionable steps based on real-life cases, this book helps you transition into your own definition of retirement. An essential and empowering read in our ever-changing world.

—Philippa Gillström, *CEO, Hugging Consulting AB*

FROM
WORK LIFE
TO
NEW LIFE

FROM
WORK LIFE
TO
NEW LIFE

REWRITING THE RULES OF RETIREMENT
FOR SMART PROFESSIONALS

MIKE MISTER &
REBECCA HILL

ACADEMY
PRESS

For permission requests, write to the below address:

PYP Academy Press
141 Weston Street, #155
Hartford, CT, 06141

The opinions expressed by the Author are not necessarily those held by PYP Academy Press.

Ordering Information: Quantity sales and special discounts are available on quantity purchases by corporations, associations, and others. For details, contact the author at rebecca@wisesherpa.co.uk.

Edited by: Nancy Graham-Tillman
Cover design by: Nelly Murariu
Illustrations by: Yao Chen Chuang
Typeset by: Medlar Publishing Solutions Pvt Ltd., India

Printed in the United States of America.
ISBN: 978-1-955985-21-5 (paperback)
ISBN: 978-1-955985-22-2 (hardcover)
ISBN: 978-1-955985-23-9 (ebook)

Library of Congress Control Number: 2021920242

First edition, January 2022.

The information contained within this book is strictly for informational purposes. The material may include information, products, or services by third parties. As such, the Author and Publisher do not assume responsibility or liability for any third-party material or opinions. The publisher is not responsible for websites (or their content) that are not owned by the publisher. Readers are advised to do their own due diligence when it comes to making decisions.

The mission of the Publish Your Purpose Academy Press is to discover and publish authors who are striving to make a difference in the world. We give underrepresented voices power and a stage to share their stories, speak their truth, and impact their communities. Do you have a book idea you would like us to consider publishing? Please visit PublishYourPurposePress.com for more information.

 PYP Academy Press
141 Weston Street, #155
Hartford, CT, 06141

DEDICATIONS

Syndi, Olivia & Stephanie

James, Maddie, Anne, Ron and Elizabeth

ACKNOWLEDGEMENTS

We have been assisted by a small tribe of friends, colleagues, and advisors who have helped us bring what started as thoughts anchored in our experiences into the polished form you are reading today. To Jenn T Grace and all at Publish Your Purpose for encouragement and guidance, and especially Bailly Morse for keeping us to the timeline. To Nancy Graham-Tilman for editing in record time and Nelly Murariu for magicking up the super graphics. To Rob Lees, Iain Maclean, and Dr Donna Johnston who provided invaluable, voluntary editing of our early drafts and Ron Hill for doing the final proof—thank you!

We are also indebted to a host of collaborators: Kevin Doolan, Richard Macklin, Henry Marsden, Ori Wiener, Toby Hoskins and Joanna Corr, Professor Nigel Spencer, Andrew Wright, Tony Crossley, Jack Crumlin, John Lucy, Peter Melrose and Professor Ashish Nanda and Professor Adrian Furnham, Dr Donna Johnston, Stephen Denyer, Liz Gray, Liz Bingham, Jill Pay, Susan Goldsworthy, Kalpa Patel, Jan Babiak, Louise Chester, Lesley Salem, Margot

Von Aesch, Eve Read, Beth Knight and Philippa Gillstrom. Thank you also to Elizabeth Isele, Helene Martin-Gee, Rick Torseth, Chip Conley, Joanna Santinon, Bina Mehta, Shaheena Janjuha-Jivraj, Lena Chauhan, Joanne Cumper and the Big It Up team, Fleur Bothwick OBE, Natasa Nikolic, Michelle Settecase, Sharon Burrell, Rick Torseth and the TCL tribe, Yvonne Sonsino, Becks Armstrong, Pippa Hopkins, Ella Marriott, Kathleen Murray, Julia Hobsbawm, Valerie Boakes, Claire Miller and Lindsey Bowser for all their support, good humour, and sound advice.

Inevitably, we will have omitted some names from these lists, and this is omission on our part and no slight is intended. If this applies to you, please accept our humble apologies and very grateful thanks.

Finally, we are indebted to the many hundreds of executives with whom we have had the pleasure and privilege to work. Their good humour, openness, and bravery—and willingness to immerse themselves in trying new things in pursuit of building a new reality and rewarding encores for themselves—has been an ongoing source of wonder and inspiration. We thank you most sincerely.

This book started life in the Four Corners Café in Waterloo, in London, UK, when face-to-face meetings and coffee with friends and colleagues was so much easier than in later 2021. We realised that the global health pandemic would cause many people to consider their options, reflect on their possible futures, and revise their plans. We hope, in some small way, this short volume will be of help.

CONTENTS

PART 2
KEY CONSIDERATIONS

CHAPTER 7

PART 3
MAKING IT HAPPEN

FOREWORD

This is YOUR time!

As a wise person we know once said, most business books tend to be 300+ pages because printers need the spine to be big enough for the title and stores want books to be attractive on their shelves! We question whether that's a good place to start. Besides, is quantity really better than quality? So, we have written this short and concise, highly practical book for mid- to later-career professionals looking to transition out of large organisational life and to whom the traditional "rules" of retirement are no longer that attractive or relevant.

Working with many professionals over time, we have discovered that it is easy to become stuck when heading into or in the midst of this major transition. The process of reflection and self-awareness is vital, but many professionals end up lacking inspiration as to where and how they can forge their fulfilling encore careers. They need encouragement to experiment, play, make mistakes, and learn. That is what this book provides.

Though this book is concise, it packs a punch. You can read it in a single afternoon or carry it with you on a journey. It provides you—the transitioning professional—with inspiration and provocation for experimenting with the first steps towards building an impactful, purpose-led encore career. Whilst this may not seem urgent, our experience is that many face it once it is too late to kick start the process. The tools in this book are for you to use, adapt, or ignore, but the key is to have fun, experiment, and be bold!

Mike Mister & Rebecca Hill

PART 1

OVERVIEW AND INTRODUCTION

CHAPTER 1

OUR STORIES

The two of us first connected on the idea of Encore Careers for experienced professionals when working for a leading global consulting organisation. There we were developing a roadmap for experienced leaders in the business, particularly those in the final stages of their organisational life and career. At the same time we were evolving as professionals, edging closer to our own encore careers. As we moved into this space, both with our work and in our own professional journeys, we became increasingly fascinated by why some professionals thrive and others struggle. Sadly, some even go into rapid decline as they transition out of large organisations into post-organisational life. Over many conversations we conceived and formulated the basis for this book: a practical roadmap for professionals who want to reinvent retirement and thrive in their encore careers.

Our own journeys are ones of long careers in large organisations, building expertise, and climbing the ladder of success. However, in our late-40s and mid-50s, respectively, we decided that our encore careers were calling us and made the bold decision to move on from large organisational life. We were not ready to go into any form of early retirement as might have been the case only a decade or so earlier. So how did we approach it and what did we learn?

As you will see from our individual stories, our journeys were distinctive, and yet they share common themes. Based on our years of experience collaborating with high achieving professionals in both our organisational lives and now as consultants, we consolidated these themes and created interventions and programmes to help professionals successfully transition into their encore careers. We have been asked repeatedly whether we have a book. So, this is our attempt to synthesise and bring to life a highly practical written guide for helping successful professionals like you transition into fulfilling and purposeful encore careers. We hope you find it a useful tool for navigating this exciting yet daunting step in your journey!

REBECCA'S STORY

In the heady mid-'90s, I started as a keen graduate in the City of London, working in financial publishing—interestingly the only role that offered me a final salary pension. I rapidly moved through a succession of marketing and business development roles in global professional and financial service organisations, including a three-year stint in Paris. In 2005, I joined one of the "Big 4" accounting firms, working my way to a global director role specialising in people-focused business strategy and organisational change. During this time,

I developed well-honed intrapreneurial, coaching, mentoring, and facilitating skills.

After almost 25 years in the City, I made a break for it and plunged into the entrepreneurial space. Having successfully launched several ventures with my business and life partner, James, I set up my company Wise Sherpa at the end of 2019 where I work as a trusted advisor, thinking partner, and consultant with impact- and purpose-led organisational leaders. I am particularly interested in working with experienced and mature professionals seeking to transition out of large organisations and pursue the next phase of their careers and lives.

At the core of my belief system, I have a passion for the economic empowerment of women. I am particularly proud to have led EY's Global Women. Fast forward Programme and have continued to take an active role in the UK delegation to the Women20 (W20), an official engagement group of the G20 which works to advance women's economic empowerment across the G20 nations.

I have an MSc in Coaching and Consulting from Saïd Business School, University of Oxford, and HEC Paris and am a Chartered Marketer and qualified coach.

I am also a very committed and hands-on (and at times exhausted) parent to our daughter. I have lived and worked in several countries including France, the US, and Switzerland but consider myself a European at heart; I spend a month every summer in the South of France in our campervan.

Looking back over the past 25 years, I see where key trigger points in my career intertwined with my personal life and influenced the decisions I made. They clearly set me on different paths (some good, some not so good), but ultimately led me to where I am today: a portfolio professional, entrepreneur, working parent, impact investor, spouse, board member, writer, coach, mentor, elder caregiver, thinking partner, and trusted advisor. The labels are many, but I am integrative and fulfilled in my approach.

Like many I know, as I look forward, I struggle with labels and am finding it liberating to be able to be the pluralist I have always wanted to be. I am led by my sense of purpose, curiosity, and desire for positive impact and legacy.

MIKE'S STORY

After joining a major professional service firm mid-career (a job I thought was only going to last a couple of years), I realised that 22 years of my career—and life—had sped by with hardly any recognition on my part.

My early career started in retail banking, and I managed to enter the world of HR via a stint as a project manager in the defence industry and a secondment to a major development charity. These experiences, and a couple of personnel directors who had given me chances, provided the all-important first job experience that broke the "Catch 22" faced by too many people trying to make a career move: you can't get a job because of a lack of experience, and you can't get experience because you don't have a job. The chances I had been afforded enabled me to break that cycle and move on to new and diverse undertakings in the HR world.

When I first entered the world of professional services, it took me a while to realise I had joined a firm stuffed full of smart, intelligent people. It was a firm where I was allowed—no, expected—to act on my own initiative. I had to play my part in a community of professionals within a joint and several liability partnership and adapt to everything that the culture entails. It became all-consuming. The lines between work, social life, and home all became increasingly blurred. After 10 years in global headquarters my final incarnation came with extensive travel, hectic, fast-paced schedules, world class education and development, and an international network of professionals as my colleagues and friends. I realised then that I was a very different person from the one who had joined up all that time ago. Outwardly, I had all the trappings of a successful career as an international road warrior executive. Inwardly, it raised uncomfortable questions: *So, is this it? What else is there? And, more worryingly, What do I do now? I am, after all, supposed to be a grown up and be able to make decisions about these sorts of issues for myself. What do I do now?*

So, after 22 years of mostly "purple patches"—those great times in a good market doing terrific work with wonderful people—I emerged, blinking, into the outside world. To my surprise and horror 22 years of my life really had passed. I began to realise that I had become semi-institutionalised, and that my world was defined and encompassed by the firm. This presented a rather large and very worrisome question: *What was I to do now that I was fast approaching a time of life when an enforced "retirement" was looming and if I did not take control, others would start making decisions for me.*

The answer presented itself during a conversation with some former colleagues who invited me to join their firm. This led to introductions by my co-authors and opportunities for writing and consulting with ingenious people. At the same time, I was trying to find work that accommodated the various strands of my life—any one of which had the potential to become overpowering!

MAKING THE CONNECTION

Through sharing our stories and backgrounds, our intent is to offer you insights into the experience we have gained. We have practised critical observation during our work with professionals transitioning out of large organisational life into their encore careers, and we now apply it here to help your transition be less intimidating and even exciting. Providing a roadmap for your professional and personal fulfilment, we illustrate the art of the possible and enable informed decision-making when it comes to your encores. To get the most out of the book we recommend you take the time to really engage with the content, reflect, and complete the exercises.

CHAPTER 2

SETTING THE SCENE

You may be a professional in the private sector such as an accountant, lawyer, consultant, physician, engineer, surveyor, HR/talent recruiter, IT expert...the list is long. Or you may be an experienced professional in the public sector such as the armed forces or civil or public service. Across all of these, we increasingly see professionals leaving organisations much earlier than before. It is not unusual now for professionals to retire in their early- to mid-50s, whether by choice or not.[1]

We also observe that many experienced professionals do not feel ready to follow the traditional route of retirement; indeed, many are keen on or potentially need to remain economically active with purpose. Many baby boomers and early Gen X[2] professionals are "non-digital natives," meaning

---

[1]Across the G20, one in three workers is aged 50 and over, and this is set to increase to four in 10 by 2040 (Sourced: International Longevity Centre).

[2]The workplace currently comprises several generations. For our purposes, we define these as the following: Silent Generation (Born 1945 or before); Baby Boomer (Born 1946 to 1964); Generation X (Born 1965 to 1976).

they have not grown up with technology but had to learn how to use it in adulthood. These professionals are likely to be unsure of what their options are and how to manage a life transition of this magnitude. As professionals they may have spent most of their careers inside one or two organisations, so the transition into an encore career is a significant challenge due to lack of experience managing such changes. Some may be fortunate enough to be offered coaching and/or outplacement support for the transition, but this can pose difficulty because much of the support offered is focused on finding another full-time role. Many professionals may not wish this and/or may struggle to secure another full-time role. An often-neglected issue is that of ageism in the workplace; many professionals feel pushed or eased out before they are ready. And yet, there is so much exciting opportunity for those who seek to explore and embrace the change beyond organisational life.

Our collaboration on this book represents both the baby boomer and Gen X perspectives, provides both male and female insights, and allies our experiences with a strongly commercial viewpoint. We believe the motivations of, and potentially the choices available to, these groups are different. Gen X is more likely well into their 50s to have school-aged children, and baby boomers are more likely to be empty nesters. Both groups are likely to have elder care responsibilities. Our experience shows us that women are more likely to consider or be forced into this move earlier than their male counterparts who may well be trying to avoid or put off the inevitable for longer. We aim to bring together these different perspectives and highlight what we hope will be a truly inclusive roadmap, recognising and acknowledging the different motivations and needs of individuals.

Some of the factors affecting your choices

CHAPTER 3

YOUR CAREER AS A PROFESSIONAL

Many professionals will likely spend their careers in a small number of organisations where they will have plied their trade or profession as an accountant, a lawyer, a consultant, an architect, a surveyor, or in some other capacity. Their work life is based upon advising clients using their knowledge and experience. The raison d'être for most professionals is taking a deep dive into testing their own capabilities and knowledge by using their wisdom and skills in the service of solving problems. Their working life, certainly in private practice, is in the company of similarly smart people with a comparable drive for excellence. A less kind analysis would say that it is a narrow, siloed existence with a fairly homogenous group of colleagues and clients.

For most professionals, their career trajectory will have been a stratified apprenticeship in which skills are acquired through often serendipitous experiences that are layered on to the day job of being a practicing professional. The ever-present need to deliver fee-earning revenue is often times paramount, but on the way the professional will be asked to undertake some low-level recruitment or organise functions or marketing events. As they progress in their careers, they may be asked to lead internal projects, an office reorganisation or similar tasks, all while maintaining their levels of utilisation, fee earning, and technical proficiency.

However, it is an exceedingly rare thing for these professionals to be called upon to reflect on the experiences they are having and to formalise their reflections into what they have learned for future benefit. And we should remember that many professionals have never been formally trained in project management, finance (unless they are accountants), marketing, or human resource management. Nevertheless, it is a common occurrence for professionals to lead and manage multi-million dollar/euro assignments across many borders and distances. These projects and programmes are crucial and risky for organisations, but they are often entrusted to individuals who have had no formal training in the core disciplines needed for successful execution.

This is in sharp contrast to the typical career route in a major corporate entity. As soon as promotion or progression is deemed appropriate, an individual in the corporate world is usually provided with management and leadership development support. The aim is always to assist them in the progression from individual contributor and team member to supervisor, manager, and leader. This presents a curious paradox: Progression in a corporate setting usually means relinquishing most skill sets and knowledge for which one was originally hired. Yet this is supplanted by the fact that corporations help employees acquire knowledge and skills for expertly getting things done within the organisation itself. Professionals such as lawyers, accountants, doctors, architects, and surveyors tend to focus their career interests on being accomplished professionals. As such, many do not accord skills in project management, team leadership, organisational leadership, or staff motivation as being of real value. The trouble is that in their new, in all probability, post-organisation world, these are the very skills that are most useful and valuable—and dare we say, can be easily monetised.

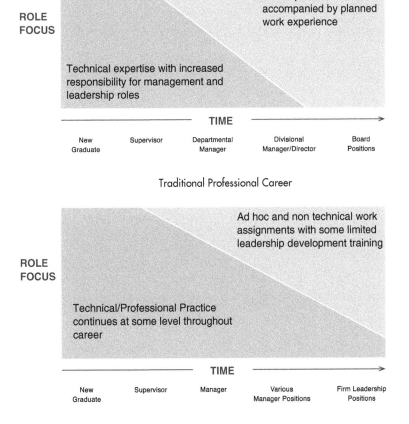

Traditional Corporate Career

ROLE
FOCUS

Increasing quantities of Managerial & Leadership Development activities accompanied by planned work experience

Technical expertise with increased responsibility for management and leadership roles

TIME

| New Graduate | Supervisor | Departmental Manager | Divisional Manager/Director | Board Positions |

Traditional Professional Career

ROLE
FOCUS

Ad hoc and non technical work assignments with some limited leadership development training

Technical/Professional Practice continues at some level throughout career

TIME

| New Graduate | Supervisor | Manager | Various Manager Positions | Firm Leadership Positions |

CHAPTER 4

THE 100-YEAR LIFE— TAKING AGENCY AND HAVING A PLAN

The research is clear, and the evidence base is growing: our lives are longer than those of our ancestors,[3] and for many of us, increasing with every generation. However, we cannot assume that just because our lives are extending in duration that the quality will be better than that of our ancestors.

Here is what we do know about our lives as we go headlong into the twenty-first century:

1. How they evolve depends considerably on our socioeconomic circumstances and our access to education and opportunities. In addition, gender, ethnicity, cultural

[3]Office for National Statistics (ONS)

background, sexual orientation, and health all play significnic roles.

2. How these factors play out and impact our professional lives influences how we may view and approach the idea of a 100-year life.[4]

3. We will work until we are older, either by choice or need. Traditionally, where we would have retired in our mid-60s (or even earlier), we now anticipate many choosing or having to work into our 70s and 80s.

4. Work and life will increasingly integrate. Working remotely will become the norm.

5. Career "gaps" in which individuals are "on-ramping" and "off-ramping" will be increasingly common as individuals prioritise relationships, life-long learning, health, and wellbeing. The care of self and others will increase the need to take time out as will the need to retrain or upskill in order to stay relevant.

6. Mastering the art of career transitions will become a critical part of a professional's skillset as the number of transitions we expect to make during our lives increases.

7. The range of jobs on offer will increase in variety and will move from a permanent employee model to what we currently call a "gig" economy model. This means professionals will be expected to have a much broader and evolving set of skills (e.g., digital marketing, sales, networking) as well as the ability to deal with change and uncertainty.

---

[4]Lynda Gratton and Andrew Scott, *The 100-Year Life: Living and Working in an Age of Longevity* (London: Bloomsbury Publishing, 2016).

8. The choices we make regarding how we value money and time will evolve and shift.
9. Ultimately, we will expect to live out our lives with purpose and impact.

> *Purpose is the deep well that always has water.*[5]
> —Nick Craig

It is the latter point that we see as highly significant to encore careers. The power of purpose and its role in longevity is the subject of a growing body of research. In a recent study undertaken by the University of Michigan School of Public Health, researchers analysed data from 7,000 individuals aged 50+ years. Results indicated that stronger purpose in life was associated with decreased mortality.[6] Strikingly, these same researchers also found that individuals whose responses reflected a lack of purpose were more likely to die sooner than those who had self-organising life aims that stimulate goals. In this same study individuals without a purpose were more than twice as likely to die earlier than those with one. Critically, purpose it would appear seems to be more indicative of longevity than gender, race, or education levels, and more important for decreasing risk of early death than quitting drinking and smoking or exercising regularly. The research also indicated that any purpose is better than none. The most important factor for healthy longevity is

---

[5]Nick Craig, *Leading From Purpose: Clarity and Confidence to Act When it Matters* (New York: Hachette Book Group, Inc., 2018), 5.

[6]Aliya Alimujiang et al., *Association Between Life Purpose and Mortality Among US Adults Older Than 50 Years*, Jama Network Open 2, no. 5 (2019): 1–13, doi:10.1001/jamanetworkopen.2019.4270.

simply having something that makes you excited about life and drives you.

We are increasingly aware of the need to look after our physical health as we age, but less aware of the need to ensure we have meaning or purpose in our lives as we age. Many of us can share stories of professionals we knew who, within a few years of retiring, died or drifted into old age far more rapidly than anticipated. The potential lack of purpose is not documented but could well have played a key role in their demise. They shifted from roles that gave them and the rest of the world clear purpose and identity to a life where there was little clarity of role and purpose.

We advocate that remaining professionally active for as long as you choose (and, as we will discuss further in the book, this could take many different guises through a fulling encore) is a powerful driver for healthy longevity. Reassuringly, those who feel no sense of purpose now should not despair; the study notes that it is possible to develop and evolve purpose at any stage, and this is also illustrated by some of our case studies.

The use of the word *encore* is a relatively recent development in the context of careers and is used to describe a mid- to later-life transition. This is a phase of life during which what has traditionally been considered working until "retirement" has shifted to a more harmonious blending of some form of work and personal interests. This shift leads away from the conventional cessation of work when retirees live on savings or pension with few other sources of income or activities that could be construed as "work" in the traditional sense.

In attaching the word *encore* to *careers* we describe the linking of mid- to later-life to a new, often multiple or portfolio series of interests and activities. Not all might be financially remunerative, but most are psychologically and purposefully rewarding.

Encore careers are characterised by a strong expression of living with a clear purpose and a feeling of wanting to leave a legacy or contribution. In other words, giving something back in some shape or form. For those familiar with the popular depictions of Maslow's[7] Hierarchy of Needs, the encore career could equate to Self-Transcendence that is shown as the apex of the pyramid in the diagram below. It is a place where one typically has the time, space, and experience and is prepared to allocate personal resources to achieve personal fulfilment—whatever that means to each individual.

Self-Transcendence
sense of meaning, purpose

Self-Actualization
realizing personal potential

Esteem needs
prestige and feeling of accomplishment

Belonging and love needs
intimate relationships, friends

Safety needs
security, safety

Physiological needs
water, warmth, rest

Maslow, A. H. (1967). A theory of metamotivation: The biological rooting of the value-life.
Journal of Humanistic Psychology

---

[7]Maslow, A.H. A Theory of Metamotivation: The Biological Rooting of the Value-life. Journal of Humanistic Psychology, 1967.

Stop For a Few Moments and Reflect. Take Out a Pen and Paper and Write Down Your Thoughts:

Exercise 1

- What role, if any, do you see purpose taking in your work and life going forward?
- How is this different (if at all) from your current approach?
- What actions, however big or small, can you take to be curious, explore, and experiment with your potential purpose?

Exercise 2

Using our personal stories from Chapter 1 as a starting point or guide, develop a brief statement that summarises you as a professional—past, present, and future. Have some fun—the latter part will evolve! Include your key skills or gifts. If you can, articulate your purpose as part of your statement. Don't worry if you can't; it may well emerge over time.

Another option could be to ask for input and/or share this with 2–3 people who know you well to get their feedback and help you refine further.

In the book *How Will You Measure Your Life*, the authors observe, "Frederick Herzberg asserts that the powerful motivator in our lives isn't money; it's the opportunity to learn, grow in responsibilities, contribute to others, and be recognised for achievements."[8]

Own your story—past, present, and future!

---

[8]Clayton Christensen, James Allworth, and Karen Dillon, *How Will You Measure Your Life?* (New York: Harper Business, May 15, 2012).

PART 2

KEY CONSIDERATIONS

CHAPTER 5

A CREATED LIFE— OWNING YOUR FUTURE AND AVOIDING THE DEFAULT

All the world's a stage, and all the men and women
merely players. They have their exits and entrances,
and one man [and woman] *in his time plays many*
parts.
—Shakespeare, *As You Like It*

Jacques' speech from *As You Like It* is regarded by some as one of Shakespeare's finest. It is a remarkable piece. Written 400 years before the age of modern psychology, it still resonates. Beautiful though the early parts of the speech might be, it is the latter parts that are most insightful and links us to the work of the great German American psychologist Erik Erikson[9], relevant to our exploration.

Erikson's elegantly articulated idea is that our development as humans goes through a series of eight stages from infancy to late adulthood. In summary, he suggests that as we get older, our preoccupations change and evolve.

Applying Erikson's model of the adult life cycle, in our 40s and 50s the overriding need is to generate work, ideas, people, and business. This is a crucial stage for professionals because their need is to prepare the next generation and build protégés through mentoring and coaching juniors. The goals are to influence, create, and deepen their skills beyond mastery and knowledge. More specifically, their aim is to develop wisdom, going beyond simple application of their craft to develop a depth of understanding about industries, clients, intuition, experience, and judgement.

As we reach our 50s and 60s, the idea of generativity continues to extend towards many of the same objectives, but peers start to play a much more important role as well. Our goal seems to become contributing to some sort of institutional legacy—becoming part of corporate history. We exploit our hard-won wisdom in a way that is useful to the larger corporate body while at the same time accepting our limits. In short, the issue becomes a realisation, an acknowledgement, of the integrity of our life's work.

Erikson's model strongly reflects our experiences with many baby boomers and still holds true for many Gen Xers. However, the traditional model that Erikson propounds is itself shifting and evolving as we live longer, families are

---

[9]Erikson, E.H. The Life Cycle Completed. New York: Norton 1982.

started later, and the stresses and strains of working manifest themselves differently for men and women. As a result, the interests we had in our 40s and 50s extend into our 60s, 70s, and 80s. We should recognise that these preoccupations seem to visit us naturally (increasingly sooner than later), and they still have important implications for what we do and how we work. Unfortunately, we humans are generally better at responding to change than we are at initiating it.

What do we mean by this? The message from both Shakespeare and Erikson here is clear: if we understand how our attention shifts, we should respond by seeking and initiating changes that align with these shifts. By starting to explore, reflect, and act, we make the transition to the next stage of life and career that much smoother.

CHAPTER 6

UNDERSTANDING TRANSITIONS AND THE POWER OF INSPIRATION

WHAT WE MEAN BY TRANSITION, AND WHY IT MATTERS

We frequently mention change in the context of retirement, but we believe this is doing retirement a disservice. What is likely happening is a series of major and mini transitions as you leave organisational life behind you and head into your encore.

In their book *Changing Gear: Creating the Life You Want After a Full-On Career*, Jan Hall and John Stokes explain it powerfully:

Change is about what you can see: the external behaviours that are observable, what happens on the outside. Transition happens on the inside: the emotional and personal adaptations required for sustained changed behaviour.... A transition process is, in reality, a series of multiple mini-transitions, each of which involves letting go, a degree of upheaval, and a new beginning. The process means acknowledging the good things you have achieved, but also accepting that some of your desired ambitions have not come to pass, although some of these might provide a focus for your future plans.[10]

It is also important to note that transitions can happen due to voluntary or involuntary actions, which may greatly influence how the individual approaches them.

We are particularly keen on a model of transition developed by the Modern Elder Academy (MEA) that which draws on the work of William Bridges and others to explain transitions. It is an excellent framework for understanding and navigating the journey from leaving organisational life to fulfilling an encore.

The MEA model highlights five types of transitions:

1) Personal—moving, empty nesting, divorce, strained relations
2) Physical—changing hormones, diet, sensuality, physical or cognitive health
3) Psychological—anxiety, fear, sadness, shame, loneliness, anger, depression

---

[10]Jan Hall and John Stokes, *Changing Gear: Creating the Life You Want After a Full-On Career* (London: Headline Publishing Group, 2021), 142; 148.

4) Professional—losing job/redundancy, retiring, changing careers

5) Purpose—finding legacy, spiritual connection, new direction

These transitions are not mutually exclusive, and you may, as part of the transition you are going through, be in differing phases within each type.

In his work *Transitions: Making Sense of Life's Changes*, William Bridges articulates three phases within a transition: endings, the neutral zone, and new beginnings. These are not necessarily sequential. See the diagram below for an illustration of this.

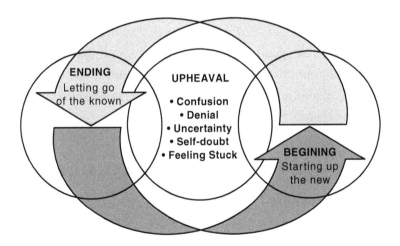

Based on William Bridges' Three Transition Phases—cited in Changing Gear[11]

[11]William Bridges, *Transitions: Making Sense of Life's Changes* (Boston: Da Capo Lifelong Books, 2004).

A common phenomenon is to get stuck within one or more transition phases, sometimes for considerable time. Fortunately, you can follow some key practices for getting unstuck. In particular seeking out inspiration, especially from those who have gone before, holds real benefit and power. Identifying and connecting with relatable role models (we elaborate more on this in Chapter 9), going into your transition with a growth mindset, and experimenting by taking small steps are other effective approaches.

Keep in mind this is not a linear process. Those closest to you may also be too close and think too fondly of you, which is why it is important to have those external voices and role models to challenge you, your thinking, and your actions or inactions. In his book *Life is in the Transitions: Mastering Change at Any Age*, Bruce Feiler notes that the average transition takes five years, and we will go through many transitions throughout our lives.[12] Therefore, there is real value in better understanding them and learning how to successfully navigate them.

The Power of Curiosity and Inspiration

In working with many professionals leaving organisational life, we find that they often get stuck either heading into or being in the midst of this major transition. As part of the process, reflection and self-awareness are vital. However, many professionals lack inspiration, and at times curiosity, as to where and how they could forge their encore careers.

---

[12]Bruce Feiler, *Life is in the Transitions: Mastering Change in a Nonlinear Age* (New York: Penguin Press, 2020), 16.

Through relevant case studies and examples, we have identified the following options commonly used by professionals when pursuing their encores. In presenting these options, we aim to encourage you to reflect, stimulate your curiosity, and inspire you to explore the art of the possible.

- Taking on Board Roles
- Applying Experienced Entrepreneurship
- Making an Impact—Mentoring, Volunteering, Investing
- Becoming an Interim Executive
- Becoming a Consultant
- Going Plural—Creating A Portfolio
- Retraining—Preparing for a New Path
- Asking "Is it okay to retire "retire"? (It really is okay to do nothing!)

To help you better understand what each option entails, we include a brief overview, key things you need to know, where you can find out more, and a case study for illustration.

Taking on Board Roles
What is It?
Most professionals who have spent time in business understand the basics of a board appointment and the distinction between executive and non-executive board positions (including independent directors).

In our experience, executive board roles typically involve working for a set number of days a month with a specific focus of supporting small- to medium-sized organisations with their day-to-day operations. This includes holding a seat on the board, which comes with formal, legally prescribed obligations and responsibilities. There are standard pay rates associated with this type of work, and the role usually requires a certain functional or industry-related expertise. In these roles, the experience you bring from your prior life is often highly valued.

Non-executive director (NED), or independent director, board roles come in many shapes and sizes. It is not unusual to start building a board portfolio with not-for-profit and/or unremunerated positions, because this can be solid ground for building skills, knowledge, confidence, and crucially, a reputation. Being vigilant and keeping a balance between unpaid and paid board positions is wise, as the number of unpaid opportunities vastly exceeds the paid ones. You might otherwise find all your available time being absorbed for no remuneration.

Whilst Financial Times Stock Exchange (FTSE), Fortune 500, or equivalent boards are the glamourous end of the spectrum, there are many board appointments available which pay, including public appointments, investment funds, and housing associations. You must consider all board roles carefully to evaluate the risks you might undertake versus the rewards you might receive.

What Three Key Things Should I Consider?

1) What is your appetite for taking risks? If it is low, then start off with roles in which there is a positive track record for organisational performance. Establish this by talking to current and past directors and industry contacts and by doing your own due diligence. This includes checking directors' cyber, professional indemnity, and personal liability insurance.

2) Board roles are like apprenticeships in that you will not know everything that is going on. Even for those who are highly experienced with boards, being on the other side of the table is an entirely different experience. It is okay to not know and to learn. Having a good set of mentors with strong board experience can help. Consider board courses if you think that would be helpful, but ultimately there is no substitute for experience.

3) Study and understand the rules of the game for obtaining board appointments and assess your own motivators and appetite for the work. Board work can be extremely demanding and time consuming, especially in high-profile organisations such as public appointments or listed companies.

How Do I Find Out More About It?

1) Reflect on your motivators for board work and where you want to put your energy and time. For example, assess the balance between paid and pro-bono work, the public sector versus the private sector, and listed versus private boards.

2) Explore board trainings and networks such as the Institute of Directors, Women on Boards, and other board certification programmes. These are particularly useful for helping you prepare your board bio/curriculum vitae (CV), which is different from your executive bio/CV.

3) Work your network. Talk to contacts who are already on boards, and target boards in which you would be interested. Be clear in articulating what you are looking for and what you have to offer. Consider contacting search and selection consultants—colloquially known as

headhunters. Each headhunter will have a different focus, so you may need to spend time targeting the right ones. Check out relevant publications where board roles are advertised, including online boards. For example, some to check out in the UK are *The Third Sector*, *The Guardian*, *The Times*, and *The Cabinet Office*.

4) Research and talk to as many board members and individuals as possible who can offer insight. Always keep an eye on the risks and rewards—board chairs can be very seductive and flattering to the ego. But is the risk-reward ratio right for you?

5) Be patient; it takes time.

Typically, most board appointments last about three years with a maximum number of three rotations. As you build your board portfolio, best practice is to start a new one, work on one mid-term, and complete one as the term comes to an end. Having at least three portfolios is advisable, but this does depend on your motivations and capacity for work.

Mary's Case Study

Now leading a very successful encore career as a board director for a number of major international corporations, Mary "side hustles" as a coach and mentor for executives transitioning into board positions and for senior executives working with their boards. Her current situation is the culmination of years of experience and hard work in a variety of roles, together with a powerful drive and personality that have enabled her to build a rewarding and successful encore.

Mary's early career started at a major international professional service firm. Achieving partnership at a relatively young age (she confesses to be a very driven individual who at 8 years old already had a 10-year plan), she realised that her partnership deed stipulated she would need to leave the partnership by the time she turned 60. This raised the question of how to manage her career for the next 25 years. To provide herself with a path, Mary built the first of what would become 10 year-rolling career plans.

Mary quickly identified three options that appealed to her: she could develop sufficient experience to leave the firm and become a CEO of a mid-cap organisation, she could become an entrepreneur and build her own scaling business, or she could build a portfolio of roles. So, she set about acquiring a skill set and gaining experience that would allow her to follow any one of these paths.

To this end, as her career in professional services progressed, Mary undertook ever larger and more challenging business and leadership roles. On many occasions the roles offered did not align sufficiently with Mary's three possible destinations, but "A plan is only something to help you compare opportunities," she would say. She used the opportunities these new roles presented to acquire skills such as increasing her profit and loss, executive recruitment, and business leadership responsibilities and build her network of contacts for the future. Mary was able to forge links with Search and Selection Consultants, attend and teach training and development programmes, and meet and interview board directors and chairs.

For a variety of reasons, Mary decided that she would make her big career transition at age 50 instead of 60 as she had originally envisaged. Ultimately, Mary wanted more choices and control over her work. It was time to move—but which of the three options was most appealing?

For her, the choice of board work was the preferred option because it aligned with her values and offered her the most control and choice. It also allowed her the opportunity to be involved and advise across the breadth of issues facing a business. She swiftly put her plan into action to find roles, building on and benefitting from all the relevant experience and relationships she had established.

Over time, Mary refined her criteria for accepting a board appointment. Outside of the usual financial and legal due diligence required, she summarised her criteria in this brief list based on her interest and experience:

1. Is technology going to be important to the organisation's success?
2. Is the company international in scope?
3. Can I and will I be "allowed" to contribute?
4. Will this be "good" for humankind; is the company doing something positive that will make a difference in this regard?
5. No "jerks" There is no need to work with people who are obnoxious.

In terms of formal due diligence for board roles, Mary undertook extensive desk research, including analysis of analyst reports and investor briefings, statutory filings, and social media searches and research on the other board members as well as for the company's competitors. This meant spending up to three weeks for research while striking a balance of showing enough interest to keep the opportunity live and avoiding being seen as too "needy." Additionally, interviewing the company and being interviewed by the company were equally important tasks.

Looking back, Mary considered her first role on a board as a trial and waited for almost two and half years before finding and accepting the "right" second role. The delay was partially a result of contemporaries cautioning that she was "too much of an operator," so it seemed wise to make sure that the role was what she actually wanted. After all, her transition preparation did provide other career options. Fortunately, that first role worked out well and led to a second, much higher profile appointment which started the ball rolling on others.

Mary's main advice to individuals who are interested in board director work is, "Be intentional. There is a lot of supply and relatively little demand, especially for board work, so you need to find clarity in what you are seeking to do and use that direction to drive action."

What Else Should I Consider?

If you are keen onboard work, build on Mary's insights and consider five criteria you will use when exploring and deciding on which board director roles to apply for. To inspire you, we have included a few questions that should help guide you towards those five criteria:

- Is this a passion project or do I want to be paid for it? How much time and effort do I want to put towards finding board director roles and doing the work?
- From a values and interest perspective, what type of organisations am I interested in, and which ones should I avoid (e.g., environmental impact, tobacco, arms)?

- Which sectors am I credible in? How can I demonstrate my credibility?
- As a board director, what expertise do I have that will ensure I can contribute effectively to the board agenda and discussions?
- What steps do I need to take now, and in the time I have, to line myself up for board director roles?

Where Do I Start?

In our experience, there is no substitute for identifying and talking to individuals who are leading successful, plural careers by managing their time, energy, and finances based on the objectives they have set for themselves.

In addition, there will inevitably be a variety of regulatory and legislative implications to taking on board roles. So, most jurisdictions will have an "Institute of Directors" or equivalent body which will probably offer some type of formalised training and development and possibly even certification. Almost certainly there will also be some sort of sector or trade body that represents the organisations in each sector. It would be worth spending time investigating their websites and membership requirements and generally researching the specifics for the sector(s) in which you are proposing to work.

Finally, review and evaluate the roles we have highlighted when deciding on the optimum mix for you and consider accessing the relevant resources for those roles.

Applying Experienced Entrepreneurship
What is It?

Looking at media today, the pervasive image of entrepreneurship is young hipsters and the cult of youth. Yet research tells us that the most successful (i.e., those who are still in business profitably after 5 years) are individuals aged mid-40s and older.[13] There is a compelling case for experienced professionals to become entrepreneurs when they can make use of their wealth of knowledge and accumulated experience to pursue a passion or interest.

To be clear, this is not about taking your previous profession and becoming a self-employed freelance version of your former self. This is about having an idea and a vision for a business that you can grow and evolve. It is about becoming a business founder and owner using a personal driving force to exploit your knowledge, networks, and experience to fill a customer need for a product or service. Entrepreneurship is not necessarily for those who are looking to achieve a certain lifestyle balance, because it is likely to be all-consuming, frustrating, and financially challenging. Yet it can also be exciting and extremely rewarding.

What Three Key Things Should I Consider?

1) The highs and lows of entrepreneurship are well documented. Personal resilience is the trait most entrepreneurs list when asked what the key to their success has been.

2) Having a clear vision and motivation for the business is critical for ensuring you stay connected and do not lose sight of your goals.

3) Identify your financial model and expectations for the business and yourself. Ask yourself whether you can afford the time lag between creating the business and receiving the first revenue. Some business ideas require

---

[13]Kauffman Foundation—CEO presentation 2016.

substantial financial investment and often this must be externally raised. You can find very quickly that you are no longer the key decision maker in your own business.

How Do I Find Out More About It?

With the evolution of digital technology, the entrepreneurship ecosystem has rapidly evolved over the past 20 years. With a myriad of online resources such as podcasts and blogs giving insight and providing guidance, it is now easier than ever to become an entrepreneur. There is, however, no substitute for exploring your network, especially any professional alumni network(s) you can access. Figure out who inspires you in the way they lead their business and secure time to speak with them. Figure out who your tribe is. For example, if you want to be a social entrepreneur with a business focused on delivering social impact, seek out different organisations linked to social entrepreneurship.

Katherine's Case Study

Katherine spent the greater part of 25 years building her career in professional services, working across several different business units and making her way up the ranks in sales and marketing. Latterly she led large strategic change projects.

Where once she loved the full-on nature of her work—travelling extensively, regularly changing teams and leadership roles, forging into unknown territory—in her mid-40s Katherine found herself increasingly frustrated with her work life. Keeping up with the required level of commitment proved overwhelming, especially in conjunction with her commitments outside of work; she had a young family and a husband who was setting up a business on his own.

Whilst still working full-time, Katherine gradually became involved with her husband's new enterprises. She helped him set up not just one but two different businesses and enjoyed the challenge. She could see how he was thriving as an entrepreneur and wondered if this might be something that she could do.

Using her experience as a qualified coach, she set out on a journey of reflection and experimentation. Quite early in this process, she left her full-time role. It was a daunting decision, but Katherine knew it to be the right one for her.

She had an idea that she wanted to continue to help her husband build his business, and they became partners. She took longer, however, exploring whether she might also build her own business and what that could be. As a purpose-led individual, it was important to her that her business reflect this. The process was and continues to be highly iterative.

Katherine's approach focused on speaking to a broad range of individuals. She contacted associates from her previous work life, friends and colleagues from her MSc and community of practice, and various professional networks she belonged to over the years. She also sought out some professional coaching. She experimented with the startup space but quickly realised that her interest and future was more about collaborating with people than about the process. She completed several carefully selected courses, investing considerable time and money upskilling herself, and this was interlinked with exploring and experimenting with varying degrees of success.

Three years into the entrepreneurship journey, Katherine has now reached a point of greater clarity. She continues to be involved with her husband's business as a co-owner and is slowly building her own consulting organisation, blending the needs of being an entrepreneur with her other priorities. As she heads full-on into her encore career as an experienced entrepreneur, Katherine has identified what type of colleagues and clients she wants to work with and the impact she wants to have.

What Else Should I Consider?

- If you are keen on entrepreneurship, build on Katherine's insights and ask yourself what this might look like for you.
- Do you want to run a business based on your previous experience or embark on an entirely different journey, sector, and focus?
- What idea do you have that fulfils an unsatisfied need or gap in a consumer market?
- Would you prefer to be a sole owner/founder or co-founder, have a lifestyle business, be part of a scalable business with employees, or buy into an existing business or franchise?
- What do you need to know or learn in order to make the move?
- To whom can you talk to help you explore this further?

Entrepreneurship shares some characteristics with being a consultant, so refer to the advice in that section.

Where Do I Start?

Entrepreneurs tend to welcome and seek out like-minded fellow "travellers," so it should be fairly easy to track down other entrepreneurs. Typically, you can find entrepreneurs clubs online, and many universities and academic establishments host innovation centres (check out Google Garage). Local governments tend to support local enterprise initiatives, so it is well worth checking with local chambers of commerce or your local equivalent. With a wealth of materials online, the key is to find an entry point into a community of entrepreneurs. This will connect you with others who have similar challenges and interests.

Making an Impact—Mentoring, Investing, Volunteering
What is It?

We often find that individuals at this stage of their lives are strongly motivated by the desire to make an impact by leaving a legacy in some way. This could take many guises, but here we focus on what we have identified as the three most common.

First is mentoring. Harvesting your years of professional experience and finding ways that it may be of service to future generations in the form of mentoring can be extremely rewarding and stimulating. A popular approach is to align yourself with an educational institution which requires mentoring support for its students. These usually include MBAs or Masters students but could also extend into secondary or other mainstream education. Another way is to align yourself with an interest. Many organisations support business owners, founders, and entrepreneurs through mentoring if they have substantial sector or industry experience. An example of this would be the New Entrepreneur Foundation which helps high-achieving graduates build and scale businesses. Organisations like these are often referred to as "accelerators," and you can find them quite easily through local business support networks (e.g., regional growth hubs which in turn may be looking for industry mentors).

Second, and allied closely with mentoring, is the opportunity of active investing. Oftentimes, mentors end up becoming investors in organisations they are mentoring. There is also the possibility of taking up an active investor role by exploring organisations through which you can join a consortium that offers training in investing and where you group together to invest. One growing interest in the impact investing space is investing for good. By this we mean investors who are motivated by broader societal, environmental, and community benefits and not just financial return.

Third, volunteering can also be an incredibly rewarding activity. Many individuals choose to do this as part of a group of activities rather than exclusively dedicating their time to it. Voluntary board work can be a good place to start if you are looking to build a board portfolio. Other experienced professionals choose to volunteer in order to help their local communities in such areas as school literacy and numeracy schemes. One benefit of volunteering is you can ramp your volunteering commitments up or down at your discretion.

The one thing all these approaches have in common is that they are effective ways of building and extending your network. In turn, this becomes part of the self-fulfilling cycle that fosters other endeavours.

What Three Key Things Should I Consider?

1) Typically, mentoring work is unpaid, but it often initiates valuable connections and leads to other opportunities. Be clear on your motivations for engaging with these activities. As you progress further into the work, check in

with yourself on a regular basis to make sure that your experiences are delivering against your motivations and expectations.

2) A note of caution though, it is quite easy to fill your time with these activities, especially when they involve causes and institutions about which you feel passionate. As this work is usually pro-bono, it sometimes happens that the value you contribute is not fully recognised by the institution, and there might be times when you can be taken advantage of. Therefore, it is up to you to ensure you set boundaries and adhere to them.

3) Investing carries risk, and you need to be fully engaged in understanding and managing the process if you pursue this path.

How Do I Find Out More About It?

For mentoring, a good place to start is self-study. A great deal of information is available on the how and what of mentoring. We have highlighted above several avenues to potentially secure mentoring roles; however, there are many other ways to obtain mentoring positions. Getting the word out to your network is another effective way to start. Encore. org is an exciting new organisation founded in the US which is developing an innovative approach to inter-generational mentoring and could provide a blueprint for the future. The organisation runs regular virtual taster sessions for more information.

When it comes to investing, a good place to begin can be with Angel Investing associations. In the UK for example, the British Business Angels Association acts almost as a trade body for various networks and consortiums.

The remarkable thing about this approach is that you do not need any experience; the association provides support and training. Reaching out through your network will likely also provide a rich seam of opportunities.

When it comes to volunteering, it helps to have an idea about the type of voluntary work you might like to do and the sort of organisation you want to work with. For example, the UK has many organisations that focus on young people's literacy and numeracy for those who are interested in the issue. You can also check the National Council for Voluntary Organisations or the Charities Commission in the UK. Both charities have a registry of organisations that might be relevant to you. Another place to look is in publications, such as *The Third Sector*, which advertise a variety of volunteer opportunities. Ultimately, much of this type of work is about local community connection and the value that you derive from being part of a community. Roles or opportunities tend to be shared through local networks, so make sure to be proactive in seeking advice and council from your local community. If you are interested in knowing more about becoming a magistrate or school governor, check online for relevant local resources.

Jill's Case Study

As the first ever female Serjeant at Arms at the House of Commons, Jill was never going to be able to "retire" quietly. Caught in a whirlwind of exit events, she was very conscious about not sounding repetitive when asked to say a few words about her unique professional experience and her impending "retirement." In preparation for these talks, she reflected on her life, both professional and personal, and three strong themes emerged as pillars to most of her work: supporting and mentoring professional women (including female colleagues) wherever possible, ensuring children had access to the best learning opportunities (including work experience), and entrepreneurship. Having had grandparents and a mother who were all entrepreneurs, she helped and supported small- and medium-sized enterprises (SMEs) wherever she could. Most importantly, she did not arrive at these pillars or core values by looking into the future but rather by reflecting on her past and deciding to embrace them as the basis for her future focus.

As she left her high-profile role, Jill wanted to spend her time making a difference across the three pillars she had identified. Initially, she volunteered as a reading helper in a local primary school for Beanstalk, one of the UK's major children's literacy charities. She was soon asked to be one of their trustees and later took on the role of chairperson. When Beanstalk merged with a much larger charity, Coram, she was asked to join their board. At the same time, Jill was asked to join the board for the Shakespeare Schools Foundation, chair the senate of a leading professional women's network, Savvitas, and lead a key workstream on data in the All Party Parliamentary Group on Women and Enterprise. In turn, this led to a role as a non-executive director on the board of a revolutionary artificial intelligence company focused on data in this space.

Looking back, Jill is clear that she wanted to "retire" while she still had the energy, health, and enthusiasm to continue making a difference. Whilst she did do some part-time consulting and board advisory work in the first few years after leaving her organisational life, she also spent those years building up her impact portfolio. When she initially left her organisation, she recognised that she had anxieties about how she would manage the transition financially. Consulting work most definitely helped ease her into what she refers to as her higher purpose, impact-focused work (not to say she did not find purpose in her consulting work). Jill notes, "You can do as much or as little as you feel able to commit to. You can also experiment and see what works and what doesn't. The freedom is that you are doing what you want to do, not what other people want you to do."

On an ongoing basis, having the three clear pillars of women, children, and entrepreneurship helps Jill create and evaluate opportunities as they arise in her impact work. She always starts with the question, "Can I make a lasting change here? And if yes, what would it look like?" She describes the feeling of freedom, flexibility, and having an impact as the greatest of gifts!

What Else Should I Consider, and Where Do I Start?

Whether they are in mentoring, investing, or volunteering, your networks must be recognised and understood. Identify where you have gaps and start addressing them. Nearly all opportunities in the impact space come through personal connections. Do not let this put you off; use your time wisely to develop your networks before leaving organisational life.

Also spend time reflecting, identifying, and understanding your basic principles, values, or drivers centred around the impact you want to have and write them down. Use them as your reference point—like a north star—as you progress into your encore career.

Becoming an Interim Executive
What is It?

The lure of a structured working environment with clarity of what success looks like lures some professionals towards more formal encore roles, even on a part-time basis. This comes with the advantage of substituting one organisation for another, often one that is slightly less high-powered but comes with the benefit of being able to focus on one specific part of their skill set. For example, an accountant in private practice moving to an interim CFO role within a smaller organisation can focus almost exclusively on financial management. They avoid having to spread their skills and time across multiple management responsibilities of a firm such as client care and delivery, team leadership, and production. For many smaller organisations, the skills and years of experience a professional brings with them are very welcome additions to their leadership team.

What Three Key Things Should I Consider?

1) Smaller organisations may not always have the budget to hire full time. Be clear on your expectations surrounding payment and required work, as scope-creep (those occasions when more work is either needed or expected to complete a project but there is no increase in the fees) is not unusual in this situation. Beware: old habits die hard, and many professionals succumb to overdelivering in these situations. You might find that though you are contracted for three days work, you end up spreading that work over five days. For some professionals this works well, but this is usually because they have negotiated and hold to the agreement.

2) Though it can be an attractive proposition to work in this capacity, it is helpful to have a timeframe in mind for transitioning to what comes next or to line up your next assignment.

3) Recognise that this is an approach that requires some planning and good networking. Proactive networking is the name of the game when it comes to this type of work. Building productive and ongoing search and selection consultant (headhunter) relationships and a strong social media presence may also be some things to consider as part of this approach.

How Do I Find Out More About It?

Contact headhunters who usually have a dedicated practice for interim appointments. There is also a strong interim community which tends to cluster on social media. LinkedIn can be a good starting point for research. Do not forget that if you belong to an industry association, it might be a useful resource for tapping into these opportunities. Then, of course, there is your own network. If people know you are looking, then they are more likely to help and alert you to opportunities within their networks. The more specific you can be about what you want, the easier it is for them to help.

Liz's Case Study

After a successful and largely rewarding career as a partner in a major consulting and accounting business, Liz was feeling increasingly burned out by the demands of the organisation and the work. She could feel her confidence and sense of self starting to take a hit, and in her words, "It was very scary." But what to do? After much deliberation and in some ways trying to put off "the day of reckoning," Liz decided to take the leap and see what presented itself. She knew that she had more left in her to contribute professionally, so retiring into a life focused mostly on leisure was not going to work for her.

Liz had always been active in one of the major industry associations attached to her profession, ending up as president in the years preceding her exit from a large organisation. She had a strong network across her profession and beyond. She was not necessarily looking for interim roles, but when the board of the association she had been president of approached her to see if she would be interested in an acting/interim CEO role for one year, she decided to go for it. This role extended by an additional six months, whereupon she was approached by another association in the same industry and asked to accept another interim CEO role—this time for a period of two years. Both her roles came with a substantial change management mandate and a small talented team to help execute it.

Looking back, Liz recognises that taking on interim leadership roles has been a necessary step in "decompression" from a full-on, high-octane career. It has given her purpose as she transitions from large organisational life. It has also allowed her to rediscover herself, have an impact in a way that is quite unique from her previous work, and explore what is going to be a rousing next stage of her life: her encore. Previously, her purpose was mostly focused on creating security through generating money and having a strong professional identity and status. Now, she has stopped planning so much and has started listening more. Liz is excited at the prospect of further exploring her untapped creativity—however it shows up.

What Else Should I Consider?

If you are a people person who likes building teams, is keen on learning, and has strong problem-solving skills, you will reap considerable benefits from interim work.

Typically, organisations looking to bring in interim leadership are going through some form of crisis. Stepping into this situation as a leader to make a quick impact can be a tempting proposition. Liz advises reaching out to all key stakeholders and taking the time to listen and understand the issues before acting. She also affirms the need to negotiate up front what you believe it is going to take to get the work done. Most importantly, do not be afraid. "Have confidence to rip up the plan if that's what is needed," says Liz. There is a fine balance between being grateful for the role and being a bold, confident leader. Remember you are there for a reason.

Being self-aware and tuning into your needs is also key, especially when the time comes to wrap up the assignment. That usually happens before you are fully ready to detach in a calm and controlled way.

Where Do I Start?

Having a strong network and being known in her industry were key factors in Liz being approached for interim CEO roles. Many trade bodies, industry associations, membership bodies, and networks (both local and global) are often on the lookout for great interim leadership talent. So being proactive and reaching out to them directly is an effective route towards quality interim work. You can also work with headhunters/executive search professionals. Liz's advice is to identify a few you like and stay connected with them.

Interim roles usually have a sweet spot of tenure around 15–18 months during which time you prepare the organisation for handing itself over to a more "business as usual" form of leadership. Do not be afraid to agree upfront to upwards of a two-year role, because you can always negotiate an exit when the time is right for both you and the organisation, even if that ends up being earlier than the end of the contract date.

To be clear, though the roles are often part-time, the time you invest could be anywhere between 50 to 100 percent of the time it is said to take. Also, interim work may have a limited shelf life for both you and the organisation hiring you, but it can be highly rewarding and a great steppingstone into your encore.

Becoming A Consultant
What is It?

Consulting is about selling knowledge, skills, and advice to organisations. Based on our experience, this typically comes in two different guises. The first is continuing your prior professional life but in a self-employed or independent associates' group capacity. The second is leveraging your obtained organizational leadership experience. Effectively this means monetising your team leadership and business management expertise and skills in such areas as strategic project management, programme development, financial planning, marketing, and business development.

What Three Key Things Should I Consider?

1) Ask yourself whether you really want to continue doing more of what you have spent your professional life doing

or whether this is just the "obvious" option. What will be different if you go this route? It is all too easy to think you can do the same work for fewer hours and similar compensation. In our experience, this is rarely the case. Being a self-employed solo consultant requires you to not only sell and deliver the work but also be responsible for everything from IT setup to billing and management of your schedule or diary. Whilst you can outsource much of this, it still represents an extra demand on your time and energy. The benefit of consulting is having more autonomy over who you work with and how you work, but this does require strong boundaries and good planning because it is so easy to just slip into former working habits.

2) A good middle path could be to join with or form a small group of like-minded and trusted consultants and use this as the basis to create an associate model. An associate model consists of a group of like-minded individuals with similar or complementary skills and values who work together with varying degrees of formality and structure. Usually these are classic "eat-what-you-kill" type collaborations that draw heavily on a partnership ethos but without the structure and regimen of a membership agreement.

3) Consultants who have made a success of this approach have found a way of balancing their existing full-time occupation prior to transitioning out of the organisation. They accomplish this by negotiating reduced working hours and possible permissions that enable them to start building a client base before they leave their organisation. These professionals also spend considerable time

warming up their network regarding their move and exploring the potential for consulting work.

How Do I Find Out More About It?

Your organisation will most likely use many consultants across varying competencies, so this could be a good starting point for initial exploration. As with the other encore options, reaching out to your network can also be helpful. You may have former colleagues who have pursued this path or may be able to refer you to individuals who have done so. We have also found that it can be helpful to have role models whose approach and consulting work you aspire to replicate. You may not know them, but that does not mean you cannot contact them or at least study how they approach their work. Most solo consultants have themselves been the beneficiary of advice and counsel from those who have trodden the path before, and you will find they are typically very amenable to finding time to help others get established.

Steven's Case Study

Steven reflected that as he reached his 50s while in a professional service firm, he encountered something of a fork in the road. On the one hand was the height of his expertise, and on the other was a looming feeling that at some point he was going to leave the firm where he had spent 35 years. What to do next?

Most of Steven's partners seemed to delay thinking too deeply about this. To leave the firm meant huge uncertainty about what to do next. For Steven and his partners, the idea of simply stopping work and either playing golf or spending a lot of time with what was left of their families was an anathema. It was rare to find a partner with a clear view of what they wanted to do next. Of course, there were some exceptions—rumours of colleagues who had gone on to sit on boards, focus on charity work, and/or found something in the public sector. It all seemed very vague and was best put off for another day. After all, there were clients to serve!

Although a member of his firm's executive committee, Steven's technical skills had long been overtaken by his love of selling and proven skills as a rainmaker. But neither of these skill sets seemed to be an immediate indicator of a different future career.

Coupled to the challenge of determining a new direction, Steven had a strong feeling that if he indicated that he was thinking of leaving the firm, he ran the risk of being put in what was euphemistically called "the departure lounge." This was a space reserved for partners who were known to be leaving the firm and would inevitably be cut out of consulting with other partners on future projects and being introduced to new clients. Ultimately, "There's no point as they will be leaving soon." Not a good place for partners who have thrived on a full client portfolio.

Making a Move

Steven was fortunate in that, at a time when he needed to address his own retirement, his firm had introduced a "Pathway to Retirement" programme. The intention was to support partners in finding "second/encore careers." The plan was to build up more and more examples of success stories over time and invite these former partners back to talk about their journeys. Run over a six-month period, the meetings exposed Steven and his colleagues to headhunters, the art of

CV/resume writing, and the importance of uncovering one's needs and motivations to help choose the best-fitting next life stage.

Steven had given himself three years to plan his departure, having been counselled by the programme that he needed at least two years to plan and execute a smooth exit. He realised that there were plenty of choices open to him, but if he left too late it would become much more difficult.

As part of the "Pathway to Retirement" programme, Steven completed the Career Anchors assessment based on the work of Edgar Schein (more to come in Chapter 7). It became crystal clear to him that traditional retirement was not an option, and he had no desire to join another firm or enter mainstream corporate life as an executive. The "traditional route" of non-executive or independent directorships held little attraction either. An entrepreneurial environment was going to be vital for his going forward. The prospect of freedom and control over his own destiny with minimal commitments was looking hugely attractive. But how to make it a reality?

Earlier in his time spent at the firm, Steven earned an MBA, majoring in pricing in the professional service sector. He knew he had a body of knowledge and experience that could be monetised if he worked it into a consulting offer. Steven spent time codifying his experience and preparing, writing, and delivering conference presentations about pricing and business development. Through working his networks assiduously he was able to access positions with major business schools and conference providers, which afforded him a marketing platform for his newfound consulting offer.

Steven's encore career led to the world of consulting with law and accounting firms. His natural business development skills made him a sought-after consultant by managing partners around the world, and his reputation was enhanced by collaborating with academics at top business schools in the UK, US, and Europe. Steven is now an in-demand consultant on pricing and business development. He works internationally and frequently speaks at major conferences and events. Steven was remarkably successful in executing his robust plan in a very short time. He was focused and well-networked, and he devoted time and energy towards making it happen. Reflecting on his journey, Steven is highly satisfied with his progress and only regrets not making the move sooner. He has added about 10 years to his economic life and enjoys a feeling of immense purpose and fulfilment.

What Else Should I Consider, and Where do I Start?

Here is Steven's advice to those looking to move into consulting:

1) Talk to other consultants, especially those who have gone before you. Get yourself a really clear picture of what the life is like. It can be lonely. It can be frustrating. It can be harder work than being employed. It can also be hugely rewarding with a sense of control and satisfaction that can be difficult to explain!

2) Be clear on what your "offer" to the market will be and with whom you want to work. Who will be your ideal clients?

3) Work your networks extensively, especially the "loose ties." Most people will happily help if asked!

4) Give yourself time and a suitable financial runway to create and execute a realistic plan.

5) Consider having a "personal board of directors"—a network of confidantes and supporters who will advise and counsel you through the good times and bad.

Going Plural—Creating A Portfolio
What is It?

Historically, "going plural" meant having a portfolio of board roles. It now increasingly refers to a blend of different professional activities, both paid and unpaid. It is not uncommon to see professionals with a "business mix" of a not-for-profit, two independent directorships, and involvement in some form of consulting.

This approach is favoured by many because of its potential for flexibility and the variety it offers. Having a portfolio allows for a degree of "ramping up and down" professional activity whilst not stepping away completely, which is very attractive to many professionals at this stage of their careers. However, a word of caution: when one has ramped down, there can be a steep hill to climb when re-establishing a full portfolio (especially the revenue stream).

What Three Key Things Should I Consider?

1) The mix or formula of professional activities here is a key consideration. One example of an approach could be "one opportunity coming to the boil, one on the boil, one coming off the boil, one for fun, and one to give

something back." In practice, this translates into three business appointments in varying degrees of maturity, one activity that makes a contribution to the community, and one that is a fun thing to do. These do not have to be mutually exclusive. Increasingly, we see professionals align their activities with one pillar or theme (e.g., sustainability). So, what will your formula be?

2) Referring to your personal motivations and drivers will dictate the mix that is right for you. We consistently see time, energy, interest, and money being four key considerations when professionals choose factors that shape their formulas.

3) How good are you at placing boundaries around your professional activities and adhering to them? Having a successful portfolio of professional activities requires you to be strong with setting and managing boundaries around your time, energy, and finances.

How Do I Find Out More About It?

What we have seen work well is identifying and speaking with individuals with successful plural careers. Typically, we see professionals who are rigorously managing their time, energy, and finances based on this new objective of creating a portfolio and leading a plural encore career. You would also benefit from reviewing the various roles we have highlighted, deciding on the optimum mix for you, and accessing the relevant resources for those roles.

Susan's Case Study

After almost 25 years successfully climbing the corporate career ladder, Susan was the vice president of global communications at a large multinational corporation. She knew that she did not quite fit, and in her words she "was dancing on the edges." If she was going to continue working within a large multinational, at some stage she would probably need to change companies, and that might require another international move which was not something she or her family wanted to undertake.

For some time, Susan had been feeling a call for change from corporate life. She knew roughly the type of work she wanted to do as a change consultant coach if she were to strike out on her own. But it took her four years to take the plunge. Ultimately, the big salary and perks of corporate life were just not sufficient to balance out the inner voice challenging her.

Susan made practical use of her last couple of years in corporate by taking the following steps:

- She identified the type of work she thought she wanted to do and aligned her corporate work as much as possible to gain further experience and credentials.
- She upskilled herself by completing an MSc in Coaching and Change at the prestigious HEC Paris and Saïd Business School, University of Oxford. She felt this "validation stamp" gave her the knowledge and the network to have the confidence to make the move.
- She was already involved with an executive education programme at a prestigious management school through her company, so she used this opportunity to develop relationships and take on coaching responsibilities for one of the executive education programmes.
- She spoke to as many people as she could about their experiences with transitioning from corporate life to an encore career.

- When the time came to make the move, Susan also somewhat fortuitously negotiated a 12-month transition contract with her company. This allowed her some breathing room to build up her new portfolio of clients and work alongside her executive education coaching role.

Since taking the leap some 10 years ago, Susan has evolved her portfolio. She has co-authored three award-winning books, is finalising her PhD, and is an active member of the executive education faculty where she had originally taken on the coaching work. She is also evolving into an ecological activist. This all alongside her successful consulting practice.

What Else Should I Consider?

Here is Susan's advice to those looking to leave corporate for an encore career:

- Talk to as many people who have already done it as possible before making the move.
- Recognise that people who currently respond to you have a relationship with your role. Once you've left corporate life, they may not be that interested, so ensure you leverage your role appropriately to help you with your encore transition. To put it bluntly, you may be less useful to them in the future.
- Be somewhat thick-skinned. By making this move you will become more yourself, and that means there may be a number of opportunities you go for where your face won't fit and that's ok.

- At some point, there may be the "test from devil." The corporate world may come knocking on your door again with the "ideal" role. The litmus test will be how you feel about your encore career decision. And it's okay to want to go back to corporate.
- Relevant training is essential. Make sure you do as much of it as possible before you move.
- If at all possible, test the waters first and see if the life you envisage in your encore career will work for you. One way to do this is by going part time and building up your future career in tandem, but there are other ways too.

Where do I Start?

For those readers interested in Susan's move into academia, here are a few suggestions:

- Academia, particularly higher education and executive education, is moving away from the current model of "Sage on the Stage to Guide on the Side." What do we mean by this? Because the internet and digital technology are removing the barriers for many people, knowledge is becoming much more readily available. Therefore, academic institutions are moving to offer and provide their students and clients with a dramatically different offering. This means there are more potential opportunities for individuals who have not walked a purely academic path like us. After a successful career as a professional, you will have many of the skills and above all experience for which academic institutions are increasingly experiencing a demand.

- If you are interested in exploring academia, a good place to start is to find a middle- or lower-tier business school that would be interested in having a professional with your experience teach a module. You may not get paid, but it will be valuable experience for you to prepare a term's worth of content and develop your teaching style. It will also allow you to explore whether the academic setting is of interest to you in the longer term.

Retraining—Preparing For A New Path
What is It?

Retraining typically involves the learning and acquisition of new skills and knowledge, or possibly supplementing existing skills and knowledge, so that you are better equipped to undertake a future activity or make a radical career change. We have seen many professionals retrain in spheres as diverse as personal fitness, integrative therapy, detention, mediation and offender rehabilitation services, teaching, and tour and travel guiding. Invariably, to make a transition like this you may need to undertake substantial study and assessment; approval due to connections and prior experience is not a given.

What Three Key Things Should I Consider?

1) Start by asking yourself why you want to retrain; this is the essential starting point! Do you want to retrain because you want a new full-blown role (either full-time or part-time) and potentially a new career? Or is this to equip you for pursuing something of interest that you feel passionate about? These are not mutually exclusive! Many voluntary or pro-bono roles require you to undergo some

degree of training. Typically, this involves study and/or assessment in areas such as first aid, methodologies in literacy or numeracy, leadership skills, or police/security checks.

2) A transition such as this requires a commitment of both time and money. One option is to research any study or assessment that might be involved while still working your full-time job. Often you can negotiate study leave, and some organisations might even be prepared to assist financially as part of the transition process. This is a matter of personal choice and how openly you wish to share your plans.

3) Another option is to leave your full-time role and focus all your attention and energy on the retraining process. This, however, requires you to have a sufficient financial buffer or the means to fund such a period.

For many individuals, having a conversation or series of conversations with a coach experienced in later-life career transitions can help you test your beliefs and assumptions and offer a different perspective on the reality you see.

How Do I Find Out More About It?

If you have an idea of the sort of roles you want to retrain for, reach out to the professional body(ies) or institution(s) responsible for the training. Research and establish what their standards, training requirements, and offers might be. We do caution against making any firm commitments until you have completed your research and really understand to what you are committing yourself. Also, some bodies and individuals may inadvertently have their own prejudices.

One professional we know retrained to become a doctor in her 50s—completely self-funded. You could understand that there might be some pushback or rejection from the powers that be in such cases. Some organisations or professions may erect barriers or hindrances, but it is your career and your dreams, so do not limit them.

Reach out to your network members who can inform and deepen your understanding of your proposed retraining, institutions/professional bodies, and ensuing course of action. Explore the pros and cons from an informed insider or experienced professional and weigh conflicting perspectives. To make an informed decision, it can also help to check out employment websites such as Glassdoor and Indeed.

The old maxim "Try before you buy" is never truer than when it comes to retraining. We advocate that you consider some form of shadowing, interning, or acquiring some work experience in your chosen career path before fully committing. Ideally, this should be for more than one day and with a range of organisations because it allows you to test your beliefs and assumptions.

Kalpa's Case Study

Kalpa's career path was fairly traditional. She trained and practiced as a dentist for 25 years whilst balancing the demands of her career with raising children and caring for a large extended family. She was later headhunted and began medical negligence advisory work. The latter move appealed to her because she could see the flaws in the system and wanted to do something about it.

Once Kalpa entered the field, however, she discovered it was hard to make a difference and found the work unfulfilling, despite the great remuneration and employment conditions. She ended up taking early retirement at the age of 55. She clearly recalls the moment she took the lift to the 32nd floor of the office in which she worked. The doors opened, but she could not get out. Kalpa found herself once again on the ground floor and called leadership to confirm her decision to leave and retire.

On reflection, Kalpa saw she was burnt out. Her son had been unwell, she had been going through menopause, and what was casual drinking had escalated. (She was unaware that menopause can insidiously escalate casual drinking patterns.) The prospect of a different pace of life and spending time with extended family appealed to her.

Kalpa quickly realised that travelling and spending time with extended family was not sufficient for her. Even though she found herself in the perfect setting, she was still itching for more meaning. Being at home also proved to result in a list of endless tasks which were thankless and offered little to no validation. She missed the relationships she had at work and with her clients which provided her with validation and satisfaction: "My colleagues, friends, and family had congratulated me on my retirement and living the Life of Riley. But I hated it and felt guilty for being dissatisfied with this 'utopia.'"

Kalpa decided she had to do something, so she began volunteering with a local substance abuse service on the condition that she wanted a role with absolutely no stress. Working in reception at an addiction centre, she learnt some startling facts: substance abuse treatment has a remarkably high failure rate, and women and ethnic minorities are rarely referred to or use the available services. This led her to observe that the 90–95 percent failure rate in any other form of treatment is not tolerated, so she felt compelled to explore this further. Kalpa signed up for a year-long master's programme at King's College, London, a pre-eminent centre for addiction studies.

After the completion of her master's programme, Kalpa once again found herself at a big crossroads. What to do next? With self-limiting beliefs and the desire to remain in the comfort zone of her previous career, she felt paralysed from thinking about taking the next step. So, Kalpa engaged a career coach. With the help of the coaching, some further learning and reading, and keeping up with her voluntary work, she found her way forward. In March 2020, Kalpa decided to start a practice which provided recovery coaching for experienced female professionals with addiction issues. This was a strong social pillar of her work. Knowing that female offenders are 60 percent more likely to die in the first 14 days after leaving prison than those in the general population over the same period, Kalpa supports one woman coming out of the prison service for every paying client she receives. She is committed to working with women with trauma and addiction, because they often fall through the cracks. That is her driver. At the time of writing this book, Kalpa has no further plans to retire.

What Else Should I Consider, and Where Do I Start?

Here is Kalpa's advice for those thinking of retraining:

- Get to really know and listen to yourself again. Reach out for support. Make sure you are getting the professional support that you need to help you through the transition where needed. Personally, I found coaching invaluable as it helped me to explore and identify my purpose, determine my future direction of travel, and move to action.

- Consider exploring learning something completely new—something you may never have thought of. There are so many options now available, so be bold and brave.

- Check in regularly with yourself and those around you to share observations on how you are doing mentally and physically. This can be difficult, so ensure that you have some friends who you trust to be honest with you.

- You may experience feelings of invisibility, and possibly even stabs of regret, as the world around you continues its hectic pace. Being prepared helps. Say thank you to the multiple roles you had (professional, parent, child, caregiver, etc.), and meet the "now" you with renewed purpose, values, beliefs, and priorities.

- Dream big and lean into all the knowledge and experience garnered up to now in order to evolve into living your best life.

Is It Okay to Retire "Retire"?

In today's pressured business environment (that many of you will be part of for much of your careers), you will more than likely experience unspoken pressure to continue to be economically and professionally active. It almost seems unheard of today to decide to stop and simply devote one's time to "leisure" pursuits. But remember, after all, you can only play so much golf!

There is nothing wrong with deciding to retire completely and devote your time to family, friends, and leisure interests; pursue a passion; or add something new to your life based on a long-held, unexplored interest. But if you want to pursue this approach, ease yourself into it. Why? Ceasing all professional activity at once can be overwhelming from an identity, a personal, and a professional perspective. Some research indicates doing so has potentially detrimental health impacts.[14]

We have observed a phenomenon in which professionals who completely "retire" pick up professional activities again after a period of one to two years. Some do this with ease (usually because they have nurtured their networks), but many find this difficult.

If you do decide to retire completely, then having a clarity of purpose linked to this decision is even more important than what you actually do in your retirement. This clarity of purpose will sustain you through the transition of identity and changing relationships.

We recommend you do some reflective work on your identity. You can only be retired from X corporation or Y organisation for so long. Reflect on the following:

- Who is the new you?
- What is your purpose?
- How do you describe yourself when friends, family, or former colleagues ask? Can you answer with confidence and conviction?

---

[14]Aliya Alimujiang et al., *Association Between Life Purpose and Mortality Among US Adults Older Than 50 Years*, Jama Network Open 2, no. 5 (2019): 1–13, doi:10.1001/jamanetworkopen.2019.4270.

It is okay to not know these answers immediately. We have observed it can be useful to work with a coach on this transition, even before leaving your organisation, to explore and answer these questions. Do not underestimate the impact of this decision on you and your closest relationships.

How Do I Find Out More?

Talk to friends and colleagues who have chosen to retire "retire." Find out how they structure their time and energy and manage their sense of achievement and wellbeing.

Stuart's Case Study

Getting up is optional; Busy, busy, busy, then what?
Stuart took early retirement at 62. He was an experienced, senior HR professional who gained over 45 years of experience across three sectors: public sector, IT, and professional services. In the latter years of his career, he focused on executive learning and development, talent management, and organisational change. He saw himself as an individual with strong leadership, interpersonal, and relationship management skills. This was combined with a strong values-based, pragmatic approach to the development and delivery of business and HR-related solutions.

As he was approaching retirement, he envisioned the future a bit like a jigsaw puzzle. There were a few big pieces in place—voluntary work, travelling, spending more time with his elderly mother, etc.—which, naively, he thought was enough. Only later did he realise that there were gaping holes in the picture which somehow needed filling. Or did they? In fact, he soon realised that he could not see the whole picture.

He had to stop searching for the holy grail; it probably did not exist.

Did he need to let go of old habits and get into new ones?

Yes and no. And that is easier said than done. The main difference he found was that his habits were no longer informed by organisational and cultural norms. Without that frame of reference, he found it can be difficult because it all comes down to the individual. There is no one looking over your shoulder saying what is and what is not acceptable. Stuart had a purge on his clothes, old work papers, books, and anything else that was no longer relevant in his new world, but it left a gaping hole which only now, four years after retiring, he is slowly filling.

"I want to give something back." A laudable notion, but what?

Do something you are passionate about, not because it is there on your doorstep or because a well-meaning person thought it would be a good idea. Stuart became a trustee of his local citizens advice bureau where he was able to leverage some of his HR expertise, and he also officiates every year at the Royal Maundy ceremony in the UK. He has a caring role for his mother, now in her 90s. He wanted to be a volunteer for the National Trust Charity, but they had no vacancies—really? But he keeps looking.

We all have a moral compass. Where is yours pointing? What is your life's purpose? Find out and follow it. Stuart is still looking, and that's okay. He is enjoying life in the meantime, which is really important.

What's for dinner?

Feed the mind, body, and soul. For Stuart, breakfast became the most important meal of the day because for the first time he could actually enjoy it and take his time. He knows a healthy and balanced diet is important and has made a few adjustments. He even bought a few cookbooks—although they are still in pristine condition! As for going out, that has become even more enjoyable. Stuart enjoys finding different pubs and places to eat in areas where he has not been before.

Relationships—who needs them?

Well, most of us do. Social interaction is important; it is how we function as human beings. But do not imagine that you will keep in touch with many of your old work colleagues. Despite the best of expressed intentions, they rarely translate into anything tangible. And it does not matter. Stuart kept in touch with a few close friends from across his work spectrum, but more importantly, started to make new friends and recalibrate existing ones—including the relationship he had (or thought he had) with his wife!

"Why don't you take up golf?"

Stuart got a lot of advice, much of it unhelpful. Focus on your interests and passions, not other people's. Stuart loved travelling. He asked his wife to write down the top 10 places she wanted to visit in the UK and make a separate list for overseas. He did the same, then they swapped lists and had a conversation. There were not as many synergies as Stuart was expecting, but at least now they had a bucket list. Stuart joined a walking group with a few old colleagues from his corporate days and set up another for the people in his village.

He spends more time in the garden and is trying to be a better dad to his two sons who were largely brought up by his wife because he was spending so much time working abroad. Now he can give them the time, and you cannot put a price on that (even though 'the bank of mum and dad' has come in very handy!).

So why did he feel guilty?
Binge watching the latest series on Netflix, going to the pub at lunchtime, going to the theatre or cinema in the afternoon, having an early, early doors—whatever you are doing that is different and could be considered to be during 'working hours' might well make you feel guilty. It did for Stuart, and still does. Moving on after 45 years of organisational working life is challenging to say the least. The kudos he had gained from the many roles during a career, and the professional reputation he had built up, had now gone. And it went in an instant.

So have a plan, but do not worry if there are holes in it. That is life! Stuart just keeps going back to the jigsaw, even if it is just to look at it and reflect on what the picture might be.

In Sum

Hopefully having been inspired, challenged, and enlightened by the experiences we have presented, you are starting to think about what some of these ideas could mean for you and your encore. We do, however, share a note of caution at this point: other people's dreams and experiences can be very seductive. As you move into this next exercise, be sure to challenge yourself and explore what is really resonating and coming through for you.

Stop For A Few Moments and Reflect. Take Out a Pen and Paper and Write Down Your Thoughts:

Exercise 3

- Are there any elements of these diverse roles that resonated? If yes, which ones? Why?
- Upon leaving your organisational life, how might you explain to your family, friends, and former work colleagues what you are going to be doing? Try it on for size by practising your answer aloud in front of a mirror.
- What steps are you going to take to start making some of your ideas a reality?

> *But without purpose, life can become hollow.*[15]
> —Clayton Christensen,
> *How Will You Measure Your Life?*

---

[15]Clayton Christensen, James Allworth, and Karen Dillon, *How Will You Measure Your Life?* (New York: Harper Business, May 15, 2012).

CHAPTER 7

FUNDAMENTAL CONCEPTS

We have found the following concepts to be key based upon our experience of working with individuals going through the major life transition of leaving organisational life into fulfilling encores:

- Motivation
- Fear and Loss
- Relationships
- Money
- Time and Energy
- Business Essentials
- Technology

We invite you to reflect upon them as you work through this chapter and start to identify what steps however big or small you might take to start your process of transitioning into a fulfilling encore.

MOTIVATION MATTERS

The choice to follow a specific career path is often based on a mix of expediency, utility, and opportunism. The decision is often made without full knowledge of the enormity of the challenges that pursuing a particular career path entails. In pursuit of a career path, one inevitably makes compromises and sacrifices in the search of rewards, both material and psychological, and for advancement within the hierarchy in terms of recognition within the profession.

When the time comes to leave our organisation or end full-time employment, it is a decision of major magnitude and transition for which we are often ill-prepared. For many professionals, our work and our professions are key parts of our identity. So, making a conscious, personal decision to leave an organisation or employment potentially leaves a void in our lives. When we consider that professionals often spend a significant amount of time engaged in the profession, the complex question becomes how to fill that void and make productive use of the available time.

Edgar Schein, former professor at the MIT Sloan School of Management, proposed that we all have preferences or "Career Anchors." These are a set of talents, motives, values, and attitudes that give stability and direction to a career. Each is a combination of perceived competence, motives, and values relating to work choices. Essentially, they are elements of our self-concepts that we protect in the face of making difficult choices about how to spend time and resources.

The following summary does not do credit to Schein's work, so if you are interested in more detailed explanations of his Career Anchors, we encourage you to explore further.[16] In summary, Schein suggests we might be motivated by one or a combination of eight Career Anchors.

Technical/Functional Competence

The technical/functional competence Career Anchor relates to being good at something and working towards becoming an expert or "guru" using your expertise to the fullest. A high score in this area suggests that someone highly values the opportunity to both use their skills and continue to develop them to even higher levels. This is a Career Anchor we see often in professionals we have worked with; they feel successful when they are recognised for their expertise and have challenging work. They sometimes see the opportunity for using their skills as more important than receiving promotions and raises.

For these professionals, their sense of identity comes from exercising their skills and facing challenges within their job roles. Typically, they are not really interested in managing others and try to avoid general management, especially if it means leaving their area of expertise.

---

[16]Schein, Edgar H. and John Van Maanen, *Career Anchors,* 4th ed. (New Jersey: Pfeiffer, May 13, 2013).

Managerial Competence

Those with a high score in the managerial competence Career Anchor strongly value the opportunity to reach an elevated level within an organisation. This means they can integrate the efforts of others across functions and be responsible for the output of a particular unit within the organisation.

Emotional competence has helped these professionals become successful, and the opportunity to make decisions, direct, and coordinate work and influence others is important. They like problem-solving and working with people, and they thrive on the responsibility that comes with managing others. This career anchor is clearly related to being a generalist manager. Achieving a high managerial level in a specialist function is typically not of interest.

Autonomy/Independence

For the autonomy/independence Career Anchor, a high score suggests that someone values being able to define their work in their own way. This is another pattern we see with many professionals; those working in an organisation desire jobs that allow flexibility in how and when they do the work.

These professionals dislike organisational rules and restrictions and want to free themselves from them so they can instead determine the nature of their work without significant direction from others. They are happy working on their own and setting their own rules, pace, schedule, lifestyle, and work habits. They might also sacrifice opportunities for promotions in order to retain autonomy and a self-employment work style. (Note, this need for autonomy is different from the entrepreneurial creativity career anchor described below.) Those who prefer autonomy and independence are often attracted to careers with more freedom such as teaching or consulting.

Security/Stability

A preference for the security/stability Career Anchor suggests employment security or continuity in a job or organisation is important so that you can feel safe and secure and/or have a predictable future. Professionals who value this career anchor also value long-term prospects, locational stability, good compensation, basic job security, and community involvement. Security and Stability manifest as a concern for financial or employment security and a sense of having succeeded so that they can relax. Progression, promotion, and even the content of the work are of less importance. However, significant career achievement may be seen if roles and talents align. This may involve a willingness to do whatever is needed in the pursuit of job security over time.

Entrepreneurial Creativity

The entrepreneurial creativity Career Anchor relates to the desire to create an enterprise and run a business. This theme centres on a personal willingness to overcome obstacles and take risks without knowing the outcomes. Being creative and doing something different and new through personal effort and abilities are important motivators. These professionals also value ownership and running their own business and view financial success as proof of their abilities. Note that this is different from those who seek autonomy. Entrepreneurial creativity is about sharing the workload, but there is also a desire for personal prominence in whatever is accomplished.

Service/Dedication to a Cause

Service-orientated people are driven more by how they can help other people than by using their talents. A high score in this area suggests that the pursuit of work that achieves something of value or has a higher purpose or meaning is key. This could mean solving environmental problems, building a better world, or saving lives through the creation of new services and products. Some people will pursue such opportunities even if it means changing organisations. Promotions or appointments that take one away from this sense of purpose will likely be of little interest and hence refused.

Pure Challenge

The drive for those with a pure challenge Career Anchor is the opportunity to work on solutions to seemingly unsolvable problems, overcome difficult obstacles, and/or beat tough opposition. For these professionals, the main reason for pursuing any job or career is that it provides a forum to win out over the seemingly impossible. If something is easy, it becomes immediately boring, so they will likely move on. Thus, constant stimulation and difficult problem-solving are key elements for those rooted with this Career Anchor. Pure challenge may manifest itself in complex multifaceted situations such as consultants who are only interested in clients about to go bankrupt and have exhausted all other options or salespeople who define every sale as a win or loss.

Lifestyle

Those who are focused on the lifestyle Career Anchor examine their whole pattern of living. Making all the major sectors of their life work together towards an integrated whole is important, and they need a role that provides enough flexibility to achieve such integration. These professionals categorially do not want to have to choose between family, career, or self-development. Whilst they might be prepared to sacrifice some aspect of their career, they define success in broad terms. Their sense of identity lies with how they live their total life, where to live, their family situation, and their personal development rather than with any one job or organisation.

In Our Experience

A few observations from our experience suggest that many mid- to later-career professionals are more interested in the autonomy, creativity, service, and challenge Career Anchors. They often find that the old motivators of security (money), technical, and managerial competence no longer hold the same weight as they may have earlier in their careers. We also find that, historically, many women are interested in the lifestyle anchor throughout their careers, but that this frequently causes friction and oftentimes comes at a significant cost. This trend is starting to show with male professionals as well.

We also find that as part of the sacrifices and compromises that are made, professionals relinquish hobbies and other interests to make time for work-related activities, often defending the time allocated to work whilst at the same time trying to maintain some semblance of a life outside of work. Mid- to later-career is often a time when long-forgotten interests start to surface and professionals re-energise and address some of those long-held compromises. This can be a truly exciting time of exploration and renewal if approached in a positive way.

Having a clear understanding of your preferences helps with planning a future that is satisfying to you. You will be more fulfilled in your choices if you have some idea of your career anchors. More importantly, you can find ways of aligning with them.

Stop For A Few Moments and Reflect. Take Out a Pen and Paper and Write Down Your Thoughts:

Exercise 4

- What have been your Career Anchors to date? Why do you feel that these have been so important to you?
- How do you see these changing or playing out as you contemplate your future? Why are these changing?
- What might be the impact of these changes? What might others see in terms of changes in you and the way you operate?

FEAR AND LOSS AS BARRIERS

Many of us will have dedicated much of our lives to our work, frequently working for just a handful of employers or organisations whilst practising our professional activities. The thought of the unknown and moving away from familiarity, community (colleagues, clients, friends), and regular salary can feel overwhelming. Many professionals are unwilling to instigate career transitions or retirement and often find the decision forced or made on their behalf.

The driving emotion that underlines this reticence, whether we recognise it or not, is fear. Whether it is emotional, financial, or otherwise, we fear the unfamiliar, the uncertain, and the inability to cope or manage. Fear is a powerful force that holds us back and stops us from making decisions that could serve us favourably. This is especially true when it comes to work and our careers.

Fear, married with self-limiting beliefs such as the imposter syndrome, is incredibly potent and paralysing because we cannot see the end goal. Knowing that we want or have to leave a situation and recognising the associated costs (e.g., loss of status and salary) that are holding us back is one thing. But having clarity as to where we are headed and taking steps towards a chosen destination is another thing altogether.

Grieving (or anger or frustration) for a "lost" career can heavily deplete our energy. If you feel you are struggling to deal with the emotions, it may be useful to consider some form of support through coaching, counselling, or psychotherapy. If you do not face and work through these emotions, they may stop you from creating the future you desire and living your life to its full potential.

Based on our work, we strongly believe in the need to experiment and play with the art of the possible when it comes to options and opportunities. It is difficult, but not impossible, to have all your plans lined up before you are ready to move on. Earlier we shared with you a case of an individual who achieved this; however, our overriding experience has been that most individuals struggle with knowing they want or have to leave organisational life but not knowing how their future will look. And that is okay. The key is to recognise that your fears and self-limiting beliefs are part of the process. To understand the process and start exploring, imagine and experiment with new ideas about what you are interested in pursuing. Indulge in and get comfortable with the art of the possible.

In her book *Working Identity*[17], Professor Herminia Ibarra outlines a practical, research-based approach to playing

---

[17]Herminia Ibarra, Working Identity: Unconventional Strategies for Reinventing Your Career (Boston: Harvard Business School Press, 2004).

with and acting your way into new working identities, which is well worth further exploration and consideration. We also shared many case studies of individuals who have challenged their fears to develop new working identities and fulfilling working lives from mid-career onwards by being curious and taking action.

We have found that if you identify and name your fears, work on your growth mindset, and stay open to the art of the possible, you will be ready to experiment and will have fun. It will likely be hard sometimes but implementing tools such as compassion-based mindfulness and journaling (including gratitude journaling) and talking to a professional can help. The path may well be long, complex, and unclear at times. However, we firmly believe that you can achieve a rewarding and fulfilling life if you choose to.

Stop For A Few Moments and Reflect. Take Out a Pen and Paper and Write Down Your Thoughts:

Exercise 5

- What fears and other possible emotional barriers are impeding you from moving forward more quickly?
- What might be the impact of not addressing these fears and emotions?
- What actions, however big or small, can you take to start addressing them now?

RELATIONSHIPS ARE THE KEY

During our careers, we build a set of relationships and networks that become the basis for career advancement, getting work done, and in some cases building a social life. What successful professionals do, often without too much conscious thought, is change the shape of their networks over time to facilitate the way their careers and work responsibilities evolve.

Remarkably, when leaving organisational life, professionals often pay scant attention to the hidden assets that they leave behind: their networks. Networks are what investment bankers call an "operating platform." When questioned, many professionals cite their work colleagues, teams, and especially the junior staff with whom they worked as being what they will really miss upon leaving. Irrespective of your choice of future path, your success and wellbeing will be largely dependent upon the support network you create and nurture to help your future self and your endeavours.

Networks play a pivotal role not just in being able to get and complete work but also with regard to our mental and physical health. This makes consciously managing your networks an important task to focus on, so they align with the future life you are creating. Yet this essential activity is seldom undertaken in a conscious and ongoing manner. We have found *Who is in Your Personal Boardroom?* by Zella King and Amanda Scott[18] to be particularly useful when working with professionals. We use the authors' work to assess where

---

[18]Zella King and Amanda Scott, *Who is in Your Personal Boardroom?: How to Choose People, Assign Roles and Have Conversations with Purpose* (UK: Personal Boardroom Ltd., 2014).

the strengths and gaps might be in the professionals' networks and determine how to address them. Specifically, we look at who they need as part of their "tribe" to accompany them on this transition. Having fellow travellers/peers who are also on the journey, including some who are already ahead of it, can be extremely beneficial. This is where networks such as alumni associations or movements such as the Modern Elder Academy can help connect you with your "tribe."

A phenomenon born out of anthropology suggests we have a limit to the number of relationships our brains can manage—the maximum-sized social group is around 150 people.[19] When reflecting on our networks, we need to be aware that we only have so much "space" to devote to keeping track of and proactively managing our relationships. It follows that there will be some relationships we might foster less often (such as former colleagues). We need to ensure we have the brain space to be able to add individuals who might be new "work" colleagues, interesting contacts, or newly entered friendships.

When reviewing your work-based networks, consider past and present colleagues, suppliers and customers, sub-contractors, and people with whom you are connected through day-to-day work, training and development, and social events. Ask yourself, "With whom am I spending most of my time?" Follow that with, "Whom do I need to network and connect with in order to realise the new, upcoming life I am building?" As time is the one fixed constant in our lives, it follows that you will probably have to spend less time with

---

[19]Robin Ian Dunbar, "Neocortex Size as a Constraint on Group Size in Primates," *Journal of Human Evolution* 22, no. 6 (June 1992): 469–493, https://doi.org/10.1016/0047-2484(92)90081-J.

some of your old network members in order to be available for new people who can help sustain you in your new life. You will have to ask yourself whom will you be "moving out" or spending less time with and whom do you need to invest in to evolve. Above all, beware of a "transactional" approach—by this we mean an approach that works like a "transaction" in which you will only give if you receive equivalent "value" in return. This sort of approach will quickly burn bridges and is not conducive to the building of long term, supportive relationships. Be conscious of the loose ties you have formed over the years and do not overlook them.

When reviewing your social networks, it is easy to source additions and connections via the joint network you have with your life partner or significant other. However, we must urge using caution in exploiting this network. Those members have connected with you based on assumptions related to your joint friendships and interests. To start trying to reposition these relationships for commercial gain or other purposes will likely be met with an adverse reaction. So approach these contacts with sensitivity.

Turning now to personal relationships, dynamics are bound to shift during the transition, especially if you have a partner or spouse who is making this transition at the same time. If you are making changes synchronously, you may have much richer opportunities for discussion in the home. Still, it can be tricky to have both of you navigating such a significant transition, so it may be helpful to seek outside support in the form of coaching or counselling to ensure open dialogue.

We have observed groups of individuals who, after years of successfully working hard both professionally and in the home, choose to retire to vastly different lifestyles. For instance, one might pursue a life of golf while the other pursues professional and social activities (none of which involve golf!). We encourage you to have open discussions about your desires and plans to avert future potential conflict. Again, some outside support in the form of coaching or counselling can help keep communication channels open and conversations positively focused.

Keeping proactive discussions about the issues at hand and what each party is seeking is just as important for couples who go through these transitions at separate times. In more traditional relationships, for example, one partner might be used to occupying the domestic space for an extended time. So, they can feel as though their space has been invaded when the other partner "retires." Again, seeking outside support to help keep the dialogue open and free-flowing can be very helpful.

We have also observed gender differences in managing relationship dynamics through this transition. At this period of life, women can feel depleted in energy. Making it worse, a career shift often coincides with menopause.

Looking back over her retirement experience, Kalpa realised that menopause had played a bigger role than she had realised. Whereas before she could do things relatively easily, she found herself second- and third guessing herself on a constant basis. Her self-belief plummeted, and once that happened imposter syndrome kicked in. As Kalpa identified, the tragedy is that women are often at their most experienced and productive in these years and yet the workplace is not structured to support them. Exposure of any vulnerability is seen as a weakness. She wondered whether her decision to take early retirement might have been different had she not been going through menopause in such an isolated way.

Feelings of isolation and alienation can run high during these times, and some women are pushed into caring roles by default (now, they might still be caring for children, elders, and possibly grandchildren too). There are also significant cultural elements that play out regarding expectations of women and the roles they will fulfil in later life/retirement that need to be navigated.

Well-documented research now shows that relationships are vital for establishing and maintaining not only physical wellbeing but mental health and longevity. So much so, that even one relationship external to the home environment can make a significant positive impact on health and longevity. We encourage meticulous thought about the commitments you wish to undertake and clear communication about what you are prepared and able to take on as part of the life you are creating for yourself. To avoid feelings of frustration and disappointment in the future, it is critical to set clear boundaries. Even at the best of times, personal relationships are tricky. But through careful management and open communication, they can be successfully managed as part of this important transition. Remember, depending on what you are proposing to do with your time after leaving your organisational life, you will need to renew, change, or establish new networks and relationships. These networks will be key to finding the opportunities you seek and a source of support in the future. Nurture them carefully.

Stop For A Few Moments and Reflect. Take Out a Pen and Paper and Write Down Your Thoughts:
Exercise 6

- How might your key relationships change upon leaving organisational life?
- Who will you need to spend more or less time with?
- Where do you have gaps in your relationships and networks, and what will you do about them?

THE POSITIVE POWER OF TECHNOLOGY

Technology gives us the opportunity to dramatically review and alter our working lives. What do we mean by this? The technological revolution has reduced the "barriers to entry" for establishing a business or setting up a sole proprietorship (more to follow on this shortly). Historically, the costs would have been considerable. But now with minimal investment in some hardware (e.g., computers, printers, mobile phones), software (e.g., G Suite, Microsoft Office), and possibly some digital marketing, anyone can set themself up in business easily and relatively cheaply. However, many nondigital natives can feel overwhelmed by the prospect of taking these steps and freeze at the thought of where to start. This need not be the case.

James's Case Study

In his early 50s, after having spent a couple of years at home as primary caregiver to his young daughter, James decided to leave the automotive industry. Leaving his career in sales behind to use his acting and commercial skills to set up as an event host and moderator was something he had always wanted to do. As this was a complete departure for him, he knew he needed a website and virtual shop window to attract and direct potential clients.

Money was tight though, so his first website was built through a skill swap. James coached a web designer on her speaking and presenting skills, and she built the website in return. His major financial investments were a laptop (with large memory), printer, and mobile phone. He decided to stick with the Android platform rather than switch to Apple IOS because he was familiar with it from his corporate career. When buying his laptop, James negotiated the inclusion of the Windows Office Suite, which he needed for developing and delivering the training material he would be offering to his clients. He also negotiated 24 months' worth of antivirus software and took advantage of the free G Suite package to manage his email, documents, and work diaries. He decided that he did not need a customer relationship management (CRM) system, ultimately using Excel and LinkedIn to manage his contacts.

James realised very quickly that he needed to upskill himself when it came to using digital tools for promoting his business. By then he had managed to secure a stream of business by using his network. To assist with this, he hired a freelance social media consultant who maintained his website and social media activity. Through their collaboration, he was able to upskill himself quickly so that he could look after and manage much of the day-to-day activity himself and only pay for expertise when it was needed.

Over the years, James completed many online training modules linked to digital marketing for his business, including search engine optimisation (SEO), blogging, and vlogging (video blogging). He used platforms such as LinkedIn, Facebook, Instagram, and Twitter to target clients. Many of these tasks he chose to perform were free of charge, which allowed him to build and manage his operations on a limited budget and protect his margin. In time, James intends to outsource the social media and diary management to a virtual assistant, but his business needs to grow a little more before that becomes a viable option.

This is just one example illustrating the art of the possible when it comes to building a business you love on a minimal budget using technology to its full potential. The key is to decide what you are comfortable doing, where you need help, and how you might obtain help and keep reviewing as you progress. In the UK, for nominal or no cost, The British Business Library runs excellent courses both in person and virtually on many of these topics, as do organisations such as Enterprise Nation. See Appendices for information which lists some of the resources available for obtaining help and insight.

Stop For A Few Moments and Reflect. Take Out a Pen and Paper and Write Down Your Thoughts:

Exercise 7

1. What is the minimum hardware you will need to set up your encore (e.g., a laptop, printer, phone)?

2. What is the minimum software you will need to set up your encore? Some examples are Microsoft Office (Excel, PowerPoint, Word), document management and filing systems (G Suite), electronic diary management, virtual meeting tools (Microsoft Teams, Zoom), CRM, a financial management package, and antivirus software.

3. Do you want or need to self-manage any or all the technology, or can you outsource some or all of it?

4. What do you need to or should you outsource regarding set up?

   a. Selection, purchase, set up and maintenance of hardware

   b. Selection, purchase, set up and maintenance of software

5. Do you need a website? Do you want to outsource the building and management of a website?

6. Will you need to use social media to raise awareness of your services? If yes, do you want or need to do this yourself or can you outsource?

7. What training might be useful? How can you make this happen?

MONEY AS AN ENABLER

Let's talk about money. This book is not a tome on how to manage your finances. Financial management is way too complex a topic to discuss in detail here. It is heavily regulated and necessarily individually focused, but a wakeup call we experienced a few years ago is instructive.

In a workshop discussing life post-firm with some financially literate, smart, and savvy partners, we posed the question, "Do you know how much money you need to live on when you leave the firm?" Note the phrasing of the question: "How much money you NEED to live on." What was striking to us was that a full 80 percent of those in the room did not have an answer. Bear in mind these were financially literate people, so constructing an Excel spreadsheet with a detailed budget was not beyond their capabilities. They simply had not considered the difference between what they NEED to live on and what they WANTED to live on to maintain a certain standard of living. These two things are quite different and require attention during your planning.

Another issue is that of relativity. Many professionals earn several multiples more that the median salary in the country where they reside. It is worth taking the time to check local data regarding just what "normal" people live on. Understanding this is a great leveller, and it helps calibrate your expectations about what you really need as opposed to what you think you want.

Our key message from this brief section is that viewing "post-organisation life" as simply a financial continuation of "life in the organisation" does not make sense. Depending on the path you choose, the financial situation in your encore will be different from that of your organisational life. A realistic alignment of finances with plans and proposed lifestyle is therefore essential. And so is getting independent financial advice. To get you started, we have included a high-level tool in the Appendices.

A reputable independent financial advisor will be able to advise you on not just investments but also tendencies in life patterns such as how and when large cash demands are likely and how and when patterns of spending diminish as age advances. The financial demands of most 90-year-olds are different from those of 55-year-olds, for example, and an advisor can offer practical advice to aid your planning.

Stop For A Few Moments and Reflect. Take Out a Pen and Paper and Write Down Your Thoughts:

Exercise 8

- When will you take a careful look at your finances with your close family members?
- When will you start to draw up a "What I/we need to live on" budget?
- Have you considered speaking with an IFA? If so, when will you contact them?

NAVIGATING THE ESSENTIALS

There are many-key elements you need to consider when setting yourself up in business. Much will depend on the route you are pursuing. What do we mean by this? If you are deciding to work for yourself as a consultant, either full time or as part of a portfolio of activity, then this chapter is most definitely for you. However, if you are deciding to set up a scaling business with staff from day one, you may want to consider many of the following points, but there will be other issues you may need to add to the list due to the nature of having employees.

Another key choice which may dictate how you approach some of the following issues is whether you will set up as a sole proprietorship (SP) or sole trader, a limited liability company (LLC) or Limited Company (Ltd), a partnership, or a community interest (not-for-profit) company. Most individuals we work with choose either the SP/sole trader or the LLC/Ltd route.

An SP/sole trader has a financial cap for earnings whereas an LLC/Ltd does not. The LLC/Ltd has some additional costs and filing requirements that the SP does not. Both have their benefits and challenges. Both the UK and US government websites have excellent information on the different options available, and we recommend you spend time considering which route is most relevant for you. One point to note if you are intending to work with larger organisations is that, because there are benefits to being an LLC/Ltd, the organisation may require LLC/Ltd status as part of their purchasing procedures.

In terms of what your new working life might be like, you should carefully consider the following points we have garnered from our experience:

- *Work Location*: Where and how are you going to work? We have found that, depending on individual working styles, some professionals are quite content to work in their own space (e.g., a home office) with minimal face-to-face, day-to-day interaction (excluding video conferencing, calls, etc.). Others obtain their energy from regularly being around and collaborating with other people. Depending on where you sit within this spectrum, you may be happy working from home most of the time, or you may prefer to investigate some sort of shared working space. Recent years have seen a huge increase in the latter, and there are plenty of options from pure hot-desking to a dedicated desk set up.

- *Home Accommodations*: If you intend to work from home most of the time and you share your home with others, adjustments may need to be made to accommodate everyone. You may want to consider how, where, and when you intend to work and discuss and agree on an approach that works for all of you. This is especially important if you have previously spent large portions of the week working away from home. The impact on all parties in this transition cannot be underestimated.

- *Workspace Set Up*: If you are going to work from home, it is also wise to consider what desk/office set up you may require (including filing). There are some amazing websites now that virtually visualise the range of set ups you can consider. Again, we counsel not to underestimate the space and set up you may need. Get advice about the sort of data and files you hold and how best to store and save them for financial records, data protection, etc.

- *Specialist Services*: To operate successfully, you will need to consider what type of specialist services you may need to contract. Typically, having an accountant who can offer bookkeeping services can be a good start. There is plenty of online finance software now that simplifies this process. For a small monthly or annual fee, you can use the software to track all income and expenditures so that your accountant can easily reconcile and create the necessary return. And if you decide to register as an LLC/ Ltd, your accountant can also complete your director and sales tax/VAT returns.

- *Legal Advice*: You may also wish to obtain some legal advice for any key documents you need when setting up. Typically, a standard contract for your services includes Terms and Conditions, a Non-Disclosure Agreement (NDA), a Privacy Policy, and a pro-forma invoice (although the latter could be part of your online finance software). These are all useful to have when setting up. An increasing number of online service providers also have standard legal documentation that you can either download for a fee or subscribe to on a monthly or annual basis.

- *Data Management*: This is one of the more challenging parts of operating your own business. If you are handling any data and are UK based, you will need to register at the Information Commissioners Office. There is an annual fee for doing this, and you will need to ensure that you are compliant with the European General Data Protection Regulations or any subsequent or complimentary regulations applicable to the way you manage data. Other jurisdictions may well have similar legislation; we advise checking. Again, there are now many excellent online resources available where you can obtain help and guidance.

- *Insurance*: You will need some form of insurance to cover your business activity, most likely including professional indemnity, public liability, directors and officers and cyber. Fortunately, there are many new entrants in this space, so it is worth shopping around and finding a good option for your business. If you are taking on any board or public appointments, ensure there is adequate directors insurance taken out by the hiring organisation on your behalf.
- *Bank Accounts*: You will need a business bank account. Again, this market has been transformed in the past few years, so there are exciting new choices out there. Some of the challenger banks have made the entrepreneur/freelance community their target client base by offering accounts that integrate seamlessly with online accounting packages.
- *Virtual Assistant*: You may also want to secure the services of a virtual assistant (VA). This has become an increasingly popular option for many consultants. Obtaining support from a VA with diary management and day-to-day administrative tasks can greatly reduce the time you have to spend on these activities, freeing you up for using your time most effectively. There is a plethora of excellent VAs in the market; the best ways to find

one are to ask around in your area and explore online forums dedicated to VAs.

- *Social Media*: Another key area where you may wish to obtain assistance is with managing your social media. This can be anything from hiring a web designer to create and manage your website (should you choose to have one), to employing a social media manager (to help you define your social media requirements and manage your social media presence) or a branding expert who can help you develop any branding you may need. There is an excellent online freelance community that can help with most of these requirements and is well worth exploring. Also, a strong VA can take on much of the day-to-day activity to help manage your social media requirements should you need it.

- *Work Sourcing*: The question now becomes how much work are you anticipating driving through social media? Some of our clients source most of their work by actively creating and sharing content via a social media presence. Others have a minimal social media presence, restricting it to sites such as LinkedIn, and prefer to source most of their work through a loose network of associates and business connections. Above all, you need a strategy to source work and identify what skills and activities you are able to take on yourself and where you may need help.

All the above points come with an attached "price tag" in terms of either your own time and energy or paying for others to help you. Through careful thought and planning, you will be able to successfully navigate these. Keeping an eye on your costs versus your time and energy is the key to success.

Always ask the question, "Where is my time, energy, and money best spent?" Managing your time and energy, trying not to do everything yourself, and recognising the parameters within which you are operating is key.

Stop For A Few Moments and Reflect. Take Out a Pen and Paper and Write Down Your Thoughts:

Exercise 9

- What sort of trading entity are you proposing to work under?
- Where, how, and with whom do you intend to be working?
- What sort of external expertise and resources will you require? How will you identify them and when will you contact them?

HARNESSING TIME AND ENERGY

Let's talk about time! Professionals are used to working hard and putting in long hours. Embracing this transition for many of us can be catalysed by the desire to have more time to do interesting, meaningful work and explore other interests and activities. However, this is a double-edged sword. When going through this transition, many professionals often fall into the trap of filling up their time and then once again find themselves overloaded and overwhelmed. We know that productivity dips after a tipping point of working approximately 40 hours a week, where time put in does not necessarily produce better outcomes. We also know that as we age, we struggle with maintaining energy. We rely, therefore, on our experience to deliver the same productivity and output in less time, and this compensates for lower levels of energy.

We encourage you to think carefully about where and how you want to spend your time:

- Relationships (family, friends, colleagues, etc.)
- Hobbies and interests
- Work (however that manifests itself)
- Wellbeing
- The unknown (adventures, new interests)

Where will you choose to spend your time in each of these activities and others that are more relevant to you?

Julia Hobsbawm gave some terrific advice to Rebecca when she worked through this transition and elaborates on this in her book *Fully Connected: Surviving and Thriving in an Age of Overload*. If you are working, you need to allocate approximately 30 percent of your time on delivery, 30 percent on business development, and another 30 percent on the necessary administration needed to run your business.[20] We believe these are incredibly useful frameworks to have in mind as you work through your transition. The idea is to create a new way of working that excites and fulfils you and not simply transition your existing ways of working to a different context. For some of you this may be your choice, but we strongly encourage you to make this decision consciously!

---

[20]Julia Hobsbawm, *Fully Connected: Surviving and Thriving in an Age of Overload* (London: Bloomsbury Business, 2017).

On this journey, managing your energy is critical. Whilst we do not intend for this book to be a wellness guide, we do find that many professionals who make this transition successfully tend to take the time to be mindful of their physical and mental wellbeing. Often this is something they overlooked for a long while. Some methods we have seen work include taking up new activities such as cycling or yoga or working with a nutritionist to get diets on track.

We encourage you to take time here to work through these ideas and share your thoughts with your spouse, close friend, or family member. You may well find that what comes out through these conversations is extremely enlightening.

Stop For A Few Moments and Reflect. Take Out a Pen and Paper and Write Down Your Thoughts:

Exercise 10

- Reflecting on the role examples we offer in Section 2, with which do you most readily identify as a possible future for you?
- How do you see yourself structuring your time and energy over a week, a month, a year?
- How is this fundamentally different from the way you are doing things now?

AND IT IS OKAY NOT TO WORK!

Amongst many professionals, there seems to be an almost unwritten rule that they SHOULD continue to work and be economically active—it is a curious form of peer pressure. For many, the urge to take a break, to do nothing, to enjoy children, grandchildren, or caring responsibilities is more important. However, after a mentally active work life, a sudden cessation or change to much less activity is a potentially difficult transition. Many professionals report that the first few weeks are great and restful, but after a while they start to long for something more. As one managing partner said, "You can only play so much golf," and as another interviewee put it, "The dog only needs walking a couple of times a day." To some this may sound dismissive, but it conveys a deeper truth.

Our advice is that doing nothing for a while is OK and should be enjoyed. However, if that urge to "do something" does become strong (even too strong), and a sense of listlessness or lack of a sense of meaning and purpose arises, then it is time to do a "stocktake." It is critical to resist the siren voices tempting you back to a slightly different version of what life was like before. We strongly advocate a period of exploring and playing to try out a variety of options and experience what a different type of life might be like. Use this time to avoid making finite, big decisions and committing to something in a fit of urgency or distress. It may take several experiments, either in a linear or parallel mode, to explore what might provide that sense of meaning and purpose that is the key to a fulfilling and long encore!

Stop For A Few Moments and Reflect. Take Out a Pen and Paper and Write Down Your Thoughts:

Exercise 11

- Is your "recuperation"/vacation time planned and time-bound? Where will you be going? What will you be doing? For how long?
- How will the end of your vacation/recuperation time morph into your new life? What will be different? What will be the same?
- What will give meaning to this new way of being?

PART 3

MAKING IT HAPPEN

We covered a lot of ground in Parts 1 and 2. Part 3 is focused on making your encore career a reality as you transition out of organisational life and get up and running!

The exercises we have asked you to complete so far relate to your motivations, experience, and skills. The templates in this section have been developed during our work with many professionals. Like you, these professionals were ready to make the move and prepared to put in the work. Keep these templates and your answers on hand as you progress on your journey.

Ultimately, the roadmap you are building must work for you. So, if a complex spreadsheet is more your style, or you prefer to keep it simple in a notebook, the decision is yours! The key is to keep focused and keep testing and experimenting. This will ensure your transition out of organisational life is successful and delivers on your expectations.

One observation we share is to start early. Complete the steps, review often, and do not hesitate to iterate and revise. This transition takes time—probably more time than you are ready to admit.

REFLECTIVE WORK

SUMMARY OF QUESTIONS IN
EXERCISES 1–11

Stop For A Few Moments and Reflect. Take Out a Pen and Paper and Write Down Your Thoughts.

Exercise 1

- What role, if any, do you see purpose taking in your work and life going forward?
- How is this different (if at all) from your current approach?
- What actions, however big or small, can you take to be curious, explore, and experiment with your potential purpose?

Exercise 2

Using our personal (brand) statements as a starting point for inspiration, develop a brief statement that summarises you as a professional—past, present, and future. Have some fun—the latter part will evolve! Include your key skills or gifts. If you can, articulate your purpose as part of your statement. Don't worry if you can't; it may well emerge over time.

Another option could be to ask for input and/or share this with 2–3 people who know you well to get some feedback and refine further.

Own your story—past, present, and future!

Exercise 3

- Are there any elements of the roles we described that resonated? If yes, which ones? Why?
- Upon leaving your organisational life, how might you explain to your friends, family, and former work colleagues what you are going to be doing? Try it on for size by practising your answer aloud in front of a mirror.
- What small steps are you going to take to start making your ideas a reality?

Exercise 4

- What have been your Career Anchors to date? Why do you feel that these have been so important to you?
- How do you see these changing or playing out as you contemplate your future? Why are these changing?
- What might be the impact of these changes? What might others see in terms of changes in you and the way you operate?

Exercise 5

- What fears and other possible emotional barriers are impeding you from moving forward more quickly?
- What might be the impact of not addressing these fears and emotions?
- What actions, however big or small, can you take to start addressing them now?

Exercise 6

- How might your key relationships change upon leaving organisational life?
- Who will you need to spend more or less time with?
- Where do you have gaps in your relationships and networks, and what will you do about them?

Exercise 7

- What is the minimum hardware you will need to set up your encore (e.g., a laptop, printer, phone)?
- What is the minimum software you will need to set up your encore? Some examples are Microsoft Office (Excel, PowerPoint, Word), document management and filing systems (G Suite), electronic diary management, virtual meeting tools (Microsoft Teams, Zoom), CRM, a financial management package, and antivirus software.
- Do you want or need to self-manage any or all the technology, or can you outsource some or all of it?
- What do you need to or should you outsource?
  - Selection, purchase, set up, and maintenance of hardware
  - Selection, purchase, set up, and maintenance of software
- Do you need a website? If so, do you want to outsource the building and management of a website?
- Will you need to use social media to raise awareness of your services? If yes, do you want or need to do this yourself or can you outsource?
- What training might be useful? How can you make this happen?

Exercise 8

- When will you take a careful look at your finances with your close family members?
- When will you start to draw up a "What I/we need to live on" budget?
- Have you considered speaking with an IFA? If so, when will you contact them?

Exercise 9

- What sort of trading entity are you proposing to work under?
- Where, how, and with whom do you intend to be working?
- What sort of external expertise and resources will you require? How will you identify them and when will you contact them?

Exercise 10

- Reflecting on the role examples we offer in Section 2, with which do you most readily identify as a possible future for you?
- How do you see yourself structuring your energy and time over a week, a month, a year?
- How is this fundamentally different from the way you are doing things now?

Exercise 11

- Is your "recuperation"/ vacation time planned and time-bound? Where will you be going? What will you be doing? For how long?
- How will the end of your recuperation/vacation time morph into your new life? What will be different? What will be the same?
- What will give meaning to this new way of being?

LIFESTYLE ASSESSMENT AND FINANCIAL PLANNING

One of the biggest changes that professionals experience during this transition is the sudden realisation that, on leaving full-time employment (even if that means self-employment in a partnership) there is no longer a regular sum of money coming in every month. Indeed, for some, the realisation that their total savings (which include pensions, property, and other investments) must last for the rest of their lives is a new source of concern. And the ultimate unknown is, "How much longer will I live?"

It has been a shock to both of us that amongst the smart, sophisticated, financially literate professionals with whom we work, there is often an absence of planning in this regard. It is almost as if this is something to be pushed back and dealt with at some future stage.

Therefore, take this short section to be an important wake up call. We encourage you to take the time to work through the following short questionnaire to assess your own needs and preparations. For every area where you have indicated a "No," decide on the action that you will take within a specific time to deal with it. Clearly this questionnaire is high-level and is in no way a substitute for the detailed financial review and planning sessions that you should hold with your financial advisor before you leave your organisation. But these critical steps will impact how you will spend your encore career.

Need	Yes	No	Actions I need to take
I know how much money I have spent, and on what, over the past three years.			
I know what I can expect as annual income in my encore.			
If there is a gap, I have a plan for additional income.			
I have had a full financial review in the last six months with an independent financial advisor.			
I have analysed where I will need to adjust my lifestyle and expenditures, and I know how I plan to do that.			
I have discussed my financial plans with my significant other and/or family members who need to know.			

Need	Yes	No	Actions I need to take
I have completed all the relevant legal documents and shared them as appropriate with family members.			
I have had a complete physical exam within the last six months.			
I have taken a hard look at my lifestyle and identified where I need to make choices.			
I have a plan for how I will stay committed to these choices.			
I believe that my current home will meet my encore needs.			
I have plans to move home and know what needs to be done.			
I feel confident that my basic needs, both from a lifestyle and financial point of view, will be adequately met in my encore.			

CAREER HIGHS AND LOWS AND KEY ACHIEVEMENTS MAPPING TOOL

This is a useful exercise to complete when you are pulling together your bio/resume/CV. It can provide insight into your key achievements, what it took to accomplish them (your strengths, skills, experience), and the impact of getting there (particularly, which achievements gave you energy).

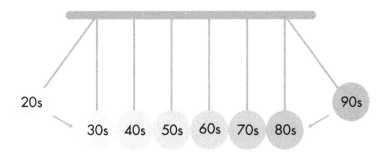

A lifetime in perspective

CAREER REVIEW

A good way to start this activity is to review your life and career in terms of decades—the momentum of your 20s accelerates into your subsequent decades until you reach a point where you can reflect back.

Try drawing a chart similar to the one below and plotting for each decade what have been the highs and the lows in terms of career, personal achievement, social endeavours, and other aspects of your life experience. For each decade, note the two or three most important achievements, write down what you have learned from them, and describe how you would explain each achievement to a stranger. Then think about how this could be added to your bio/resume/CV to provide the fullest possible picture of yourself going forward into your encore career.

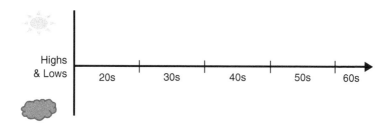

PERSONAL STATEMENT/SUMMARY

This is a useful exercise to do when preparing your personal statement. See our examples of a personal statement at the start of the book. Your brand is what you stand for and should come through strongly. It can be helpful to have your personal statement along with a professional photo on a one-page PowerPoint slide. You can share this with organisations and networks who might be interested in giving you an opportunity to give a presentation or want more background information on you.

BIOS/CVS/RESUMES

If you need a longer, more traditional bio/resume/CV and cover letter for interim roles or other work that requires them, there are many useful resources such as the LinkedIn Learning Hub. Different roles may require various formats (e.g., board bios are different from a conventional resume/CV). Also, ask HR professionals, headhunters, or recruiters in your networks to review your bio/resume/CV and cover letter and provide feedback. Typically, though, keeping your LinkedIn bio up to date is sufficient. You can also pay for external experts to help you.

OPPORTUNITY PREPARATION

If you are interested in an opportunity and have a meeting scheduled, the following questions are a starting point to help you prepare:

- What does the work/opportunity entail?
- What do you like most/least?
- What experience and training would be helpful?
- What else could you do to find out more? Any blogs, reports, articles, podcasts, publications?
- Are there any events you could attend? Which are the best/most relevant?
- Why might they be interested in me?
- Can you think of any opportunities or individuals you could link into?

PERSONAL ACTION PLAN

We have known for some time that the physical act of committing thoughts, ideas, and plans to paper or screen and sharing them through these media increases the chance they will manifest. Therefore, we have included below an action plan template for you to use to complete thorough and sustained planning. The template is structured to provide a time-framed way of approaching the planning for your transition into an encore. As we mentioned earlier, there is a need to start your planning early (18–24 months minimum, longer if you can manage it), but if you do not have a choice on timing then just start from where you find yourself today.

To maintain momentum, we also recommend setting aside dedicated time for reviewing the plan once you have researched and made contacts. This is not a "one and done" activity, but rather one that benefits from ongoing iteration and application.

Planning the last few months becomes even more important as the time approaches and the dawning personal realisation of the transitions you are making looms much closer. There will be unexpected events which others will try to squeeze into your schedule before your departure. Our advice is to make sure your departure and transition are a combination of events that you personally want to have happen and recognise that closure by way of celebration is important. Above all, keep the planning momentum going.

	18–24 Months Pre-Departure	Departure Month or 3 Months Before	6+ Months Post-Departure
Research Ideas What do I need to know more about?			
Test & Iterate Who will be a good sounding board and fierce friend for challenging my ideas and thinking?			
Develop & Execute a Plan What will I be doing, by when, and with whom?			
Monitor Progress & Adjust When and how will I review and adjust my plan?			

It is possible that the idea of forcing your ideas and plans into boxes does not work for you. If this is you, then our firm suggestion is to find another medium in which to document your thoughts. We have both spent a lot of time creating templates for the people with whom we work, knowing that templates do not work for everybody. The important thing is to move your thinking from your brain to another medium (e.g., journaling, images, etc.). If you do this, then action is more likely to follow. The questions above might help stimulate your thoughts.

A final word on planning: doing this work on your own is a great place to start, but we are strong advocates of having a "personal board of directors"—a small group of trusted advisors and friends who are also "truth tellers." They will hold you accountable for the commitments and actions you are supposed to be following. With whom will you be sharing ideas, opportunities, and plans? Who will be holding YOU accountable? Choose your advisors and your tribe carefully!

CONCLUSION

We have struggled considerably with the use of the term "retirement" in the writing process. Though the concept of retirement is changing rapidly, the word is so embedded in our language that we could not produce a reasonable alternative. In her book *The Age of Ageing Better,*[21] Anna Dixon makes the case for focusing on a more positive concept such as "Ikigai"—a Japanese word recognising later life as a time when people can pursue their passions or mission. Ultimately, we decided on the word "encore."

Having read this far, our hope is that you are excited about your encore and what lies ahead! We hope you see a wealth of interesting possibilities before you. You now have the basis of a roadmap to help guide you on your transitional journey.

Take note of our manifesto for successfully navigating this transition and creating the future you:

---

[21]Dixon, Anna, *The Age of Ageing Better? A Manifesto for Our Future* (London: Bloomsbury Publishing, 2020).

1) Start exploring different encore options (our list is just a starter). Get curious.
2) Assess your lifestyle and finances and have those important personal conversations.
3) Set some intentions and start planning. Remember to be creative, experiment, and play, and be prepared to iterate repeatedly.
4) "Act your way into a way of thinking and being."[22]
5) Nurture and work your relationships, both personal and professional.
6) Get help if you need it. Consider coaching or other professional assistance.
7) Set a date!

What will be your personal manifesto for your encore transition? We would love to know, so please feel free to share it with us via our book website or LinkedIn.

Finally, our hope is that through embarking on the journey of a fulfilling encore, you will create for those who follow a blueprint for a successful transition out of organisational life and into what healthy, rewarding, longevity looks like. So do not forget to give back to others.

You have one life. It is never too late to explore the "what ifs" to create a purposeful, impactful life and leave the legacy you desire!

---

[22]Herminia Ibarra, *Working Identity: Unconventional Strategies for Reinventing Your Career* (Boston: Harvard Business School Press, 2004), 167.

APPENDICES

A: INSPIRATIONAL TALKS AND RICH INSIGHTS

Dan Gilbert, "The Surprising Science of Happiness," filmed February 2004 in Vancouver, British Columbia, Canada. TED video, 20:40, https://www.ted.com/talks/dan_gilbert_the_surprising_science_of_happiness?language=en.

Daniel Goldstein, "The Battle Between Your Present and Future Self," filmed November 2011 in New York, NY, TED video, 15:43, https://www.ted.com/talks/daniel_goldstein_the_battle_between_your_present_and_future_self?language=en.

Daniel Levitin, "How to Stay Calm When You Know You'll Be Stressed," filmed September 2015 in London, England, TED video, 12:11, https://www.ted.com/talks/daniel_levitin_how_to_stay_calm_when_you_know_you_ll_be_stressed?referrer=playlist-the_most_popular_ted_talks_in_hindi&language=en.

Esther Perel, "The Secret to Desire in a Long-Term Relationship," filmed February 2013 in New York, NY, TED video, 18:54,

https://www.ted.com/talks/esther_perel_the_secret_to_
desire_in_a_long_term_relationship?language=en.

Jane Fonda, "Life's Third Act," filmed December 2011 in New
York and Los Angeles, TED video, 10:57, https://www.ted.
com/talks/jane_fonda_life_s_third_act#t-2848.

Matthieu Ricard, "The Habits of Happiness," filmed February
2004 in Vancouver, British Columbia, Canada, TED video,
20:41, https://www.ted.com/talks/matthieu_ricard
_the_habits_of_happiness?language=en.

Oxford Community Foundation, "Sir Muir Gray Presentation—
on Ageing and Activity with Sir Muir Gray,"
September 16, 2020, https://oxfordshire.org/insights/
sir-muir-gray-presentation-on-ageing-and-activity/.

Robert Andel, "Is Retirement Bad for Your Brain?" filmed May
2018 in Bruce, Australia, TED video, 10:58, https://YouTube.
com/watch?v=3-9WYO_MQ20&t=8s.

Robert Waldinger, "What Makes a Good Life? Lessons from
the Longest Study on Happiness," filmed November 2015
in Long Beach, California, TED video, 12:39, https://www.
ted.com/talks/robert_waldinger_what_makes_a_good_life_
lessons_from_the_longest_study_on_happiness?language=en.

TEDx Talks, "How Will You Measure Your Life?" Clayton
Christensen, YouTube, July 17, 2012, video, 19:30, https://
www.youtube.com/watch?v=tvos4nORf_Y.

B. RELEVANT BOOKS

Bronnie Ware, *The Five Top Regrets of the Dying: A Life Transformed by the Dearly Departed*
Charles Handy, *21 Letters on Life and Its Challenges*
Lynda Gratton and Andrew Scott, *The New Long Life: A Framework for Flourishing in a Changing World*
Matt Church, *The Thought Leaders Practice*

C. LEARNING RESOURCES

British Business Library: https://www.bl.uk/business-and-ip-centre#
Coursera: https://www.coursera.org/
Encore: https://encore.org/
Enterprise Nation: https://www.enterprisenation.com/
Modern Elder Academy: https://www.modernelderacademy.com/

D. RICH DATA SOURCES

APPG Longevity: https://appg-longevity.org/events-publications
Bluezones: www.bluezones.com
Centre for Ageing Better: www.ageing-better.org.uk
International Longevity Centre: https://ilcuk.org.uk/work-for-tomorrow/
Longevity Leaders: www.lsxleaders.com
Mercer: www.uk.mercer.com/our-thinking/ageing-workforce.html

BIBLIOGRAPHY

Alimujiang, Aliya, Ashley Wiensch, Jonathan Boss, Nancy L.
Fleischer, Alison M. Mondul, Karen McLean, Bhramar
Mukherjee, and Celeste Leigh Pearce. *Association Between
Life Purpose and Mortality Among US Adults Older
Than 50 Years*. Jama Network Open 2, no. 5 (2019): 1–13.
doi:10.1001/jamanetworkopen.2019.4270.

Bridges, William. *Transitions: Making Sense of Life's Changes*.
Boston: Da Capo Lifelong Books, 2004.

Christensen, Clayton, James Allworth, and Karen Dillon. *How
Will You Measure Your Life?* New York: Harper Business,
May 15, 2012.

Conley, Chip. *Wisdom at Work: The Making of a Modern Elder*.
New York: Currency, 2018.

Craig, Nick. *Leading From Purpose: Clarity and Confidence to
Act When it Matters*. New York: Hachette Book Group, Inc.,
2018.

Dixon, Anna. *The Age of Ageing Better? A Manifesto for Our
Future*. London: Bloomsbury Publishing, 2020.

Dunbar, Robin Ian. "Neocortex Size as a Constraint on Group Size in Primates." *Journal of Human Evolution* 22, no. 6 (June 1992): 469–493. https://doi.org/10.1016/0047-2484(92)90081-J.

Erikson, E.H. *The Life Cycle Completed*. New York: Norton 1982.

Feiler, Bruce. *Life Is in the Transitions: Mastering Change in a Nonlinear Age*. New York: Penguin Press, 2020.

Gratton, Lynda and Andrew Scott. *The 100-Year Life: Living and Working in an Age of Longevity*. London: Bloomsbury Publishing, 2016.

Hall, Jan and Jon Stokes. *Changing Gear: Creating the Life You Want After a Full-On Career*. London: Headline Publishing Group, 2021.

Hobsbawm, Julia. *Fully Connected: Surviving and Thriving in an Age of Overload*. London: Bloomsbury Business, 2017.

Ibarra, Herminia. *Working Identity: Unconventional Strategies for Reinventing Your Career*. Boston: Harvard Business School Press, 2004.

King, Zella and Amanda Scott. *Who is in Your Personal Boardroom?: How to Choose People, Assign Roles and Have Conversations with Purpose*. UK: Personal Boardroom Ltd., 2014.

Maslow, A.H. *A Theory of Metamotivation: The Biological Rooting of the Value-life*. Journal of Humanistic Psychology, 1967.

Schein, Edgar H. and John Van Maanen. *Career Anchors,* 4th ed. New Jersey: Pfeiffer, May 13, 2013.

ABOUT THE AUTHORS

MIKE MISTER,
BA (HONS); MBA; ACIB; CFCIPD; MBPSS.

After an early career in retail banking and the defence industry, Mike has spent most of his career in professional services, initially in the UK. He then began the serious international part of his career when he joined Ernst & Young Global in their London Headquarters in 2002. Since that time, he has worked in professional services across the world in places as diverse as India, China, USA, Australia, Israel, CIS, and across Europe and South Africa.

REBECCA HILL,
BA (HONS), MSC, DIPM, MCIM

After 25 years working predominantly in international professional services organisations leading global change programmes latterly as a Global Director at EY, Rebecca is now firmly embedded in the entrepreneurial space having successfully launched several businesses. She is currently crafting her portfolio career. Through her company, Wise Sherpa, Rebecca is collaborating with a number of Start Ups, Scale Ups, and SMEs as well as working with more established businesses as a consultant, thinking partner, facilitator, and coach working across geographies and cultures. She also sits on a range of boards and committees and is a keen advocate of Women's Economic Empowerment.

Rebecca and Mike have a particular interest and specialism working with professionals looking to transition out of the corporate world at mid- and later-careers. They consult, coach, mentor, facilitate, and speak on these issues together and independently with organisations or individuals— virtually or in person—on these issues.

Interested in connecting further with the authors?

Check out the book website: www.fromworklifetonewlife.com

You can contact Mike and Rebecca as follows or via the contact form on the website(s).

Email: mike.mister@psfi.org
Website: www.psfi.org

Email: rebecca@wisesherpa.co.uk
Website: www.wisesherpa.co.uk

Carpe Diem!